JAWS (Buchwald Version)

The great white shark swam back and forth in the Reflecting Pool in front of the Lincoln Memorial. A Democratic congressman was skinny-dipping in the pool with his girlfriend after a hard day's work. Suddenly the shark's eyes spotted the body in the water and attacked.

The frightened girl ran to a park policeman. "A shark in the Reflecting Pool just ate a Democratic congressman."

The President learned about it the following morning.

He called a meeting of the National Security Council.

"What should we do?" the President asked.

"We ought to close the Reflecting Pool," someone suggested.

"But this is the height of the tourist season," the President said. "If word gets out about the shark, no one will come to Washington."

Etc. Etc. Etc.

Washington Is Leaking

Art Buchwald

A FAWCETT CREST BOOK

Fawcett Publications, Inc., Greenwich, Connecticut

WASHINGTON IS LEAKING

THIS BOOK CONTAINS THE COMPLETE TEXT OF
THE ORIGINAL HARDCOVER EDITION.

A Fawcett Crest Book reprinted by arrangement with G.P.
Putnam's Sons

ISBN: 0–449–23294–8

Printed in the United States of America

10   9   8   7   6   5   4   3   2   1

Contents

Foreword

A tall, thin, handsome man with horn-rimmed glasses and a cigar in his mouth handed his vicuña coat to the hatcheck girl at the Sans Souci restaurant in Washington. He gave her a wink. Paul, the maître d'hotel, rushed up the steps and said, "Monsieur Buchwald, Henry Kissinger just called and said he has to speak to you."

"Not before lunch, Paul," the man said. "Not before lunch."

A hush went over the room as the man was escorted to his regular table, No. 12, along the banquette. The man always insisted on the same table so his back would be against the wall.

Gilbert, the waiter, brought a glass of iced tea. Everyone in the room pretended not to stare, but you could feel the electricity in the room.

The man then ordered his usual lunch— champignons à la grecque, a luncheon steak and petits pois, followed by a demitasse of Sanka coffee.

As the man cut into his steak, the secretary of agriculture came over to the table.

"The Soviets want a hundred million tons of wheat. What is your answer?"

"Not while I'm eating," the man said, and the secretary shrank away.

The secretary of the treasury started to walk over, but Paul stopped him. "Wait until he has had his coffee."

The secretary sat down.

Forty minutes later the man took out a fresh cigar and

lit it. Then he nodded to Paul. The maître d' escorted the secretary of the treasury over to the table.

"I need a favor," the secretary said. "The deficit is fifty billion dollars, and I only have forty billion. Will you authorize a bond issue for the extra ten?"

The man smiled. "You know I'm always good for ten billion dollars for my friends."

The secretary kissed the man's hand.

The man waved him away.

The Israeli ambassador, seeing there was no one at the table, rushed over. "You promised me a hundred F-15 fighter planes. I never got them."

The man flushed red. "Goddammit, you were supposed to have them delivered last month." The man called Paul over. "Get me a phone."

Paul brought over a white telephone with a radio aerial. The man dialed a number. "I want to speak to the secretary of defense. . . . Where the hell are the F-15s I told you to give Israel? I don't want to hear any excuses. One more screw-up like that and we go to the mattresses." He hung up the phone and said to the Israeli ambassador, "You'll have them tomorrow morning."

A strikingly beautiful girl came over and whispered something into the man's ear. He shook his head. "Not this afternoon. I've got problems at the United Nations."

With tears in her eyes the woman backed away from the table.

A short man in a gray suit came over. "Ecuador is giving us trouble. Do you have any objection if we put in a junta?"

"You know I don't like to resort to violence unless it's absolutely necessary."

"It's necessary."

"All right, but make sure no one knows I had anything to do with it."

The short man walked out without looking back.

Paul returned with the phone. "The White House is on the line."

"Tell them I'm not here," the man said, puffing on his cigar.

The Iranian ambassador came up to the table. He handed the man a five-pound can of caviar without saying a word and walked away.

Frank Sinatra walked up. "I, I, I . . . I need your help."

"Sure, kid. Anything you want."

"I want to sing in Las Vegas at one of the big clubs."

"You got it, kid."

Teddy Kennedy waved to the man from a table across the room. The man didn't wave back.

Instead Gilbert brought him the check. The man threw down a hundred-dollar bill and got up. As he walked toward the door, he nodded to a Supreme Court justice and then gave the hatcheck girl a hundred-dollar bill for his coat.

Then he walked the half block to his office and took an elevator to the thirteenth floor. He went straight to his typewriter and started to do his column. It was the only fun he would have all day long.

The Washington Triangle

THE SANS SOUCI WILL CONTINUE

One of Gerald Ford's first acts as President was to ask Paul Delisle to stay on as maître d' of the Sans Souci Restaurant. As most people know, all the important government decisions are made at lunchtime at the Sans Souci, and the President felt it was essential that in order to have an orderly transition of government no personnel changes should take place at the restaurant.

A White House aide told me, "We feel that Paul will serve us with the same loyalty that he served previous administrations. The whole world is watching what we do, and I can't think of a better way of instilling confidence than Paul remaining in this key post in government."

Many ambassadors who sat at the Sans Souci expressed delight at the news that the President asked Paul to stay on. "We don't know President Ford," one told me, "but we do know Paul, and we can deal with him. I have already cabled my government that Mr. Delisle will keep his maître d' post, and despite the changeover in government, our country can still be assured of a table."

Lawyers and high officials of the media were also pleased that Paul would stay on. One leading pundit said, "In this grave hour of crisis the country needs continuity. By asking Paul to keep his position Mr. Ford is saying, 'No matter what happens, America will survive.' "

As soon as the announcement was made, I went over to see Paul to congratulate him on the appointment.

He read a statement. "I am proud and humble that the White House would ask me to remain in office. I promise to see that nothing but the prices will change at the Sans Souci. Despite the anguish of the past year and the shock that everyone has undergone, we must never forget government officials still have to eat. We have to forget the past and look to the future. The Sans Souci stands ready to face the challenge. I will now take questions."

"Paul, it seems to me your major problem is going to be to take care of President Ford's aides who work at the White House. How will you be able to do this?"

"It will be hard at first because I won't know who they are. Unless they make the reservation in the name of the White House, I may make a mistake and turn them away, but as time goes on, I will know where the power is and adjust my reservation list accordingly."

"But can you handle all this new business?"

"I believe I can. Many of the former Nixon aides are no longer in Washington, for one reason or another, so their tables will be filled by the new regime."

"Will you still accept reservations from former Nixon people who have not been sent away?"

"Of course. They may have to wait until the present White House staff is fed, but as long as I am maître d' anyone who worked in the White House and can still afford it will be welcome. I still have customers from the Kennedy and Johnson administrations, and although they no longer have decision-making powers, they get the same food as everybody else."

"One last question. Some of the plotting of Watergate and the cover-up took place at the Sans Souci. Did the FBI ever question you about what you knew?"

"Yes, but I couldn't give them much help. Every time they asked me about someone I always replied, 'That wasn't my table.' "

LEAKS WANTED

Almost everyone living outside Washington believes that every newspaperman in Washington has closets full of classified and secret documents leaked to them by bureaucrats, congressional aides, or ex-employees of the Lockheed Aircraft Company. It's true.

Those of us who report the government's business are judged not by how much money we have in the bank but how many documents we have in the safe.

The only exception to the rule is myself. For reasons that I have been unable to explain, no one ever leaks anything to me, and it's very embarrassing to be an accredited correspondent and not have any confidential papers in my briefcase to show for it.

Occasionally I do hear from someone in the government, but I really can't call it a leak. Recently Secretary of Transportation Coleman sent me his decision on the Concorde SST, but only *after* it had been made public. Every once in a while I'll receive a hand-delivered brown envelope from the White House with a short note from Ron Nessen saying, "I thought you would like to have a personal copy of the President's speech to the Veterans of Foreign Wars." Once I showed it around at the Sans Souci Restaurant, but Dan Schorr just laughed at me.

It's really no fun at all to live in a town where everyone is dealing in secret documents and all I get is newsletters from congressmen and press releases from the "Shriver for President" committee addressed to "Occupant."

Every morning I come into the office and say to my secretary, Ellie, "Did anyone leak anything to us today?"

She always replies in a kindly manner, "No, but the afternoon mail hasn't come in yet."

I then get on the phone and start making calls. I telephone the Pentagon and say, "Do you know if anyone plans to leak anything today?" The Pentagon operator puts me in touch with a colonel. "Colonel, this is Art Buchwald, the syndicated columnist, and I was wondering if you had any confidential or secret papers you didn't want?" He always says he'll call me back, but he never does.

Then I try the CIA. "This is Beaver," I say, not identifying myself. "I want to talk to Wolf Two." I usually get a secretary. "Tell Wolf Two to meet me on the corner of Fourteenth and New York Avenue with the package." Then I hang up hoping they'll trace the call and consider me a source worth leaking to.

I see a lot of Henry Kissinger at parties, and everyone says he's the best leak in Washington. The other night Kissinger told me, "With the exception of Angola and SALT, détente is going very well." At last, I said to myself, I have something I can sell to the *Village Voice*. The question was, could I get it in the paper before Jack Anderson heard about it? But when we sat down to dinner, Barbara Howar said to me, "Henry just told me with the exception of Angola and SALT, détente is going very well." Rowland Evans and Bob Novak, who speak with one voice, said together, "Kissinger just told us that with the exception of Angola and SALT, détente is going very well."

After the dinner the parking attendant at the garage said to me, "Is it worth ten bucks to you to know what Kissinger thinks about détente?"

"Just give me my damn car," I said in disgust.

In order to get tenure at a university you have to write a book. In order to remain accredited in Washington you have to publish secret papers. I've been warned by all my colleagues that unless I come up with something soon, I will be drummed out of the Washington press corps and lose my right to be tapped by the FBI.

It's a very tough position to be put in. I hate to beg, but if anyone out there has any confidential or secret report they would like to contribute, you could save a journalist's life.

THE WASHINGTON TRIANGLE

By now everyone must know about the Bermuda Triangle, a vast body of water extending from Bermuda in the north to Southern Florida and then east to a point in the Bahamas past Puerto Rico.

Charles Berlitz, who has written a best-seller about it, claims 100 ships and planes have vanished in the area without a trace, and more than 1,000 lives have been lost since 1945.

There are many theories concerning the mystery. Some people believe that UFOs are responsible. Others feel the disasters may have been tied in with the lost colony of Atlantis. In any case, the Bermuda Triangle has caused quite a stir.

What has not been publicized is that there is a similar phenomenon right here in Washington, D.C. It is called the Washington Triangle, and it also has been a great source of mystery and unexplained disappearances.

The triangle area is located between the White House, the Capitol, and the Jefferson Memorial. Most of the accidents have taken place in the Tidal Basin, a rough, treacherous sea, five feet deep, which twists and turns as it empties into the Potomac River.

Jonathan Stone, who discovered the Washington Triangle, said, "The triangle is a frightening place. In a period of ten years we've lost thirty-four hundred trial balloons, two hundred congressional reforms, four hundred and fifty-three executive mandates, two hundred and thirty tax cuts, and one ship of state. They seem to have disappeared without a trace."

"But there must be some explanation," I said.

"The biggest disaster was the sinking of the SS *Watergate* with all hands aboard, including the President of the United States. A search of the area produced nothing but an empty lifeboat with the pathetic message 'I am not a crook' scrawled on the side."

"What do you think happened to the crew?" I asked Stone.

"They lost their moral compass. Something happens to people's sense of direction when they enter the triangle. The best political navigators forget which end is up and which end is down."

"What other disasters have taken place in the basin?"

"One day a Judge Carswell sailed out of the White House toward the Capitol to be confirmed as Supreme Court justice. Then a mysterious storm came up, and Carswell disappeared, never to be heard from again," Stone said.

"That's terrible," I said.

"Recently, President Ford sent up an energy message to the Hill and it sunk without a trace.

"At least a half dozen bills that Congress has sent down to the President to sign have drowned in the black, murky waters of the triangle. Budgets have been smashed on the rocks; campaign promises have vanished into thin air. Even a cargo of prayer breakfasts was lost without a trace or explanation."

"Do you suppose there is some supernatural power at work in the triangle that is responsible for so many disasters?" I asked.

"I'm sure of it," Stone said. "There is one theory that sophisticated beings from another planet live on the bottom of the basin and magnetically attract all the traffic between the White House and the Hill."

"I believe it," I said.

"Some say that there is a prehistoric monster in the water that eats nothing but budgets, presidential messages, government servants, and an occasional vice president of the United States."

"That could make sense, too," I agreed.

"There is also the possibility that the bottom of the Tidal Basin could be the lost colony of Atlantis," he said.

"You mean Fanne Foxe could be from another world?"

"There are many people, including respected scientists, who believe it."

HENRY IS COMING TO WASHINGTON

We're having tremendous excitement in the nation's capital this week. There is a rumor going around that Secretary of State Henry Kissinger may visit Washington, D.C. Officially State Department spokesmen are denying it. One assistant secretary told me, "There would be no reason for Mr. Kissinger to come to the United States at this time." But despite the denials, preparations are going ahead for the secretary of state's visit.

A cleaning woman at the State Department told me she had been ordered to take the sheets off the furniture in Kissinger's office, and two of Kissinger's secretaries have been seen at the hairdresser.

Painters have been sprucing up government buildings for several weeks, and Kissinger's security men have been checking out the State Department halls for the last four days.

When I confronted the assistant secretary with all these facts, he finally admitted that there was a possibility that Kissinger might indeed visit Washington. "The reason why we haven't publicized it is that Mr. Kissinger might change his mind at the last minute and fly over the city on his way to Paris. Then people would be needlessly disappointed."

The assistant secretary said that they had been making plans for the Kissinger visit for months. "He, of course, will meet with President Ford while he's here, as they have many things of mutual interest to discuss.

"After their meeting the President will host a luncheon to introduce Mr. Kissinger to other members of his Cabinet. Following the lunch we have arranged a special tour of the State Department for the secretary. Since this is such a special occasion, we plan to give State Department employees the afternoon off so they will have an opportunity to see Mr. Kissinger in the flesh. You can imagine the interest here of our people who have read so much about this man but have never seen him.

"Mr. Kissinger will then visit his office and have his picture taken seated behind his own desk. After the photos, a cocktail party will be held, where Mr. Kissinger will be introduced to foreign ambassadors stationed in Washington.

"Then we've arranged for him to go to the Kennedy Center because he told one of our people in Peking that if he ever came to Washington, he wanted to see it."

"Will Mr. Kissinger visit with the Senate Foreign Relations Committee while he's here?" I asked.

"If he's still in the country, he will. His people have warned us that he may not be able to stay for more than twenty-four hours, and since this is just a courtesy visit, they didn't want us to overbook him. We do know that President Ford has asked him to stay an extra day, but so far this is still up in the air."

"Why do you think Henry Kissinger is visiting Washington, D.C., at this time?"

"Well in the last few months he's been in London, Paris, New Delhi, Damascus, Cairo, Tel Aviv, Tokyo, Moscow, Seoul, Peking, and Vladivostok, and many people in this country felt he had been ignoring the United States. After all, we are a major power, but no one considered us one because Mr. Kissinger had never been here.

Since President Ford's personal prestige was at stake, we persuaded the Kissinger people that a visit at this time would be a feather in the President's cap. When Mr. Kissinger said he'd stop off in Washington it was, for all of us in the State Department, a dream come true."

THEY NEED A REST

The big question everyone in Washington is asking this week is: "Can congressmen chew gum and walk at the same time?" It's impossible to answer because all of them have gone on vacation for ten days.

The decision to take ten days off was not one of those spur-of-the-moment actions that the House of Representatives is noted for. It was carefully thought out and approved by the leadership.

I went up on the Hill Monday to find out what was going on while the congressmen were away.

The only one I could find, who wasn't on vacation, was a cleaning woman who had been asked to act as a liaison with the press.

After she finished mopping the floor in one of the congressmen's offices, she agreed to speak to me.

"Why would the House, after only being in session for one month, take a ten-day vacation?"

"They have to go home to make speeches in their districts telling their constituents what a mess this country is in because nobody in Washington is doing anything."

"Wouldn't it have been better if they stayed in Washington and tried to get us out of the mess?" I asked.

"Everyone needs a rest. You can't expect a legislator to work for thirty days and not get tired. When they come back from vacation, they'll be fresh and able to deal with the momentous problems of the country."

"I hate to say this, but there doesn't seem to be the

sense of urgency around here that the times would require."

"That," she said, as she squeezed out her mop, "is because you don't understand how congressmen work. They have to know what the people are thinking. They can't pass laws if they don't have their ears to the ground."

"But all you have to do is pick up the newspapers and you'll know what people are thinking. They want jobs, a halt to inflation, and some sort of tax reform."

"You wouldn't get that in ten days even if they were all here," she retorted.

"But they could get started," I protested.

She emptied out her pail in the sink and filled it with fresh water.

"If the House thought they could have done something, they would have stayed here," she said. "But since the situation is hopeless, why sit in session and fret about it? Maybe they'll get some ideas while they're skiing."

"Haven't you heard from voters who have protested the House taking so much time off?"

"There has been a lot of mail," she said, "but I haven't been able to get to it yet because I still have to mop the hall."

"Are you going to answer the mail?"

"The congressmen said I could do anything I wanted as long as I didn't break any bric-a-brac on their desks. But I doubt if I'll get to the mail. I have to see Jerry Ford at four."

"You're going to see the President?"

"He called up and said he wanted to see Carl Albert and Tip O'Neill. I told him they weren't here. Then he said he would speak to any congressman. I had to tell him they were all on vacation. So he asked me to come over to discuss congressional problems with him. I said I would as soon as I got finished dusting Sam Rayburn's bust."

The phone in one of the congressmen's offices rang. The cleaning lady picked it up. "Who is this? Senator

Jackson? No, no one is here. This is Eliza in the Rayburn Building. No, I haven't gotten around to writing the energy legislation yet, I'll work on it tomorrow. For heaven's sakes, Scoop, I've only got two hands!"

THE GREAT LEAP FORWARD

The power struggle in Washington goes on unabated and foreign ambassadors stationed in Washington are sending long cables back to their countries trying to explain it.

Here is one of the cables sent by a representative of the People's Republic of China who is living in D.C.

"Momentous historical events are taking place here in Washington with the opening salvo of President Ford's Great Cultural Revolution. At first it was believed that Henry Kissinger was behind the cultural revolution to bring disgrace on Defense Minister James Schlesinger. But now Kissinger is in disgrace himself and has been demoted to only one inconsequential post as secretary of state. He has also been cited for contempt by the People's Congressional Subcommittee. Official American newspapers are predicting he will soon be sent to North Dakota to harvest grain at a state farm run by Agriculture Minister Earl Butz.

"Kissinger is now called a revisionist and counter-revolutionary by a majority of the People's Congress for advocating détente with the Soviet lackeys in the Kremlin.

"Defense Minister Schlesinger has been exiled to the Johns Hopkins School of International Affairs in the purge and has been replaced by Donald Rumsfeld, a young member of the Ford clique who has been involved in a power struggle with the Kissinger loyalists for over a year.

"Rumsfeld has denied he was the instigator of the palace revolt, but his picture with Ford has been plastered on posters all over the outside walls of the Pentagon.

"Another victim of the purge was William Colby, director of the People's Central Intelligence Committee. Colby's main crime was that he publicly confessed to the People's Congress about antigovernment activities committed by his cadres in the name of national security.

"He is being replaced by another Ford disciple, George Bush, formerly chairman of the People's Republican Party. He was sent to China when the party fell into disgrace after Nixon's fall from power after the August, 1974, revolution.

"The biggest shock was the demotion of President Ford's Vice President, Nelson Rockefeller, who still remains in his job, but only as a figurehead with no power.

"Rockefeller, with no dissent from Ford, was accused by conservative elements of the People's Republican Party of being a counterrevolutionary bourgeois radical revisionist arrogant dog. The conservative faction led by Ronald Reagan, a former governor of the province of California, threatened that unless Rockefeller and his ilk were brought to their knees, they would see that Ford was removed from the presidency at the next People's Republican Congress in Kansas City.

"To appease this faction, Ford made Rockefeller confess to the disastrous bond crop failure of New York and ordered all photographs of Rockefeller to be taken down from the country's post offices.

"The Reagan Guard still does not seem to be satisfied with the purge. There is now a power struggle going on in the People's Republican Party over the leadership, which may be fought out between the factions in the province of New Hampshire. Be advised when President Ford comes to the People's Republic of China next month, he will be constantly looking over his shoulder to see if Reagan is standing there.

"At the moment Ford is attacking the People's Congress and blaming it for the failure of his two-year plan. He is calling on the peasants and workers to throw out the People's Democratic Party in 1976.

"How are the masses reacting to all this? So far they have refused to support Ford mainly because every time the President tries to make a Great Leap Forward, he trips over somebody's wheelchair."

A PROFILE IN POWER

President Ford has had such a big win with the American people over the *Mayaguez* incident that he has become a new man—more assured, stronger, and determined to show that the United States is not a paper tiger.

In fact, he has gotten into the habit of calling Henry Kissinger on the telephone all the time.

"Any American ships been seized lately, Henry?"

"I told you a couple of hours ago, Mr. President, if any country grabbed one of our ships, you would be the first to know about it."

"Sorry, Henry, I was chewing gum at the time. I wish the Laotians would try to board one of our vessels. I'd show them a thing or two."

"It's doubtful that any major power such as Laos is going to mess with us, Mr. President, after your strong and forthright action in the *Mayaguez* incident."

"They better not. If we show any weakness at all, every country in the world will think it can push us around. I sure wish Iceland would try to take one of our fishing vessels. I'd have the USS *Enterprise* there in no time."

"That you would, Mr. President, but it's all quiet now. Can I go back to work?"

"Henry, I was just thinking. Couldn't we have one of our ships sail close to Ecuador, maybe ten or fifteen miles out?"

"You mean in hopes that Ecuador might try to pull another *Pueblo?*"

"With this difference, Henry. We could have B-52s from Guam flying cover over it. One move toward that ship, and we drop everything in our arsenal on Quito. I will not stand for piracy of U.S. ships on the high seas."

"Well said, Mr. President. But I believe we ought to let nature take its course. There is no sense provoking an incident. I'm sure you'll have another opportunity to dramatize the unity and strength of America under attack."

"Henry, even if someone grabs a canoe, I want to hear about it."

"You will, Mr. President."

"I'd like to see Trinidad start something. We'll show them how we deal with a crisis. You don't think Trinidad would resort to piracy, do you, Henry?"

"We have no intelligence that they're thinking about it, Mr. President. But that doesn't say they wouldn't."

"Well, keep the Eighty-second Airborne on alert just in case. And I'd like some cruisers sent to Monte Carlo. You never know when Prince Rainier thinks he can push us around."

"Consider it done, Mr. President."

"Are you sure Cuba doesn't have any Soviet missiles stationed there anymore?"

"They were all pulled out in 1962, Mr. President."

"Darn."

"Look, Mr. President, I have to go back to work. I've got everyone on the lookout for any provocative act which we would have to respond to with measured force and military power. We're on top of this thing."

"You know, Henry, after the *Mayaguez* incident I received thousands of telegrams in support of my action, including one from Ronald Reagan."

"You deserved it, Mr. President."

"I get standing ovations wherever I go."

"As well you might."

"The conservatives have stopped picking on me, and even the Democrats are looking at me with new respect."

"It's a dream come true, Mr. President. But why are you so concerned to have another international incident?"

"You know how the American people are, Henry. Right now everyone is saying, 'Good show, Jerry,' but if someone doesn't grab another one of our ships, they're all going to say, 'What have you done for us lately?' "

"I LOST MY JOB"

The first thing that came to my mind when I heard about all the different changes in President Ford's "team" is what a blow it must have been to the Rockefellers.

In the last few months the Rockefellers have been throwing party after party to introduce everyone to the new vice presidential residence on Massachusetts Avenue, and it cost them a pretty penny. I'm certain they wouldn't have gone to all that expense if they had any idea that President Ford was going to push Rocky off the ticket in 1976.

As a matter of fact, I wouldn't have wanted to have been in Rocky's shoes the night he came home and broke the news to Happy.

"Rocky, you look bushed. Have a dry martini. I've been making up the guest list for our next party to show people the new vice presidential mansion."

"I wouldn't do that if I were you, Happy."

"Why not?"

"I don't think we're going to be living here much longer."

"You mean you've been fired?"

"Not exactly. But Jerry doesn't want me on his new team."

"That's awful. What are we going to do? How are we going to make a living?"

"Don't worry. I'll find something. My brother David

knows a lot of people, and I'm sure one of them will give me a job."

"How could he do it to you? You've worked so hard and you've been so loyal."

"That doesn't count when you're a vice president. Jerry's worried about his own job, and he figures if he gets rid of me, the Republican board of directors will get off his back."

"But the least he could have done was tell you before we gave all those parties. We used up our life savings entertaining the very people Jerry is trying to placate."

"Don't be too harsh on him, Happy. He hit his head on a swimming pool a few days ago, and that might have had something to do with his decision."

"Well, you can take it with equanimity, but I'm the one who has to make ends meet. We've still got the children to educate, and we'll have to move, and we still have the caterer's bill to pay."

"David will help us with a loan, Happy. It could be worse. Jerry fired Jim Schlesinger and Bill Colby today as well. We're still on the payroll until December 30, 1976. Those poor guys have to apply for unemployment insurance next week. They took one of Henry's jobs away, too."

"It's disgraceful. I think you should write Jerry a letter and tell him what you really think."

"I have to write him a letter, but I don't think I'd better tell him what I really think."

"Why not?"

"I might need him for references in case someone offers me a job."

"What I don't like about it is that he kept saying you were the greatest vice president he ever had. If he thought so highly of you, why didn't he want to keep you on?"

"Maybe it's because I'm a New Yorker. He's had it in for New Yorkers for the last six months. He makes jokes about us all the time."

"Oh, Rocky, what are we going to do?"

"I don't know. I guess you better call the caterer and tell him we may have to default on his bill."

JAWS

The great white shark swam back and forth in the Reflecting Pool in front of the Lincoln Memorial. A Democratic congressman was skinny-dipping in the pool with his girlfriend after a hard day's work. Suddenly the shark's eyes spotted the body in the water and attacked. His huge jaws clamped the torso of the congressman, who screamed once before disappearing into the depths of the pool as a pinkish red circle of blood rose to the top.

The frightened girl ran to a park policeman. "A shark in the Reflecting Pool just ate a Democratic congressman."

The park policeman wrote all the information down and at the end of his shift reported it to his superiors. The next morning his superior turned in a report to the Department of the Interior. Three days later the report landed on the desk of the secretary of the interior, who thought he'd better make a report to the White House.

The President learned about it the following morning. He called a meeting of the National Security Council. "What should we do?" the President asked.

"We ought to close the Reflecting Pool," someone suggested.

"But this is the height of the tourist season," the President said. "If word gets out about the shark, no one will come to Washington."

"Yet if we don't act and another Democratic congressman gets killed by the shark, they might accuse us of a cover-up," an aide pointed out.

"I think the first thing to do is to find out how the shark got there. Does anyone know if the CIA put a shark in the Reflecting Pool?" the President said.

The director of the CIA replied, "If they did, it was

without my permission. I'll call the shark division to make sure."

The director came back in a few moments. "They say it wasn't them. And they don't think it was Howard Hughes."

"The Soviets wouldn't put a shark in the Reflecting Pool, would they?" the President asked.

"Not while the SALT talks are going on," the secretary of state said.

"Sir," the aide said, "it's our responsibility to alert Congress that there is a shark in the Reflecting Pool even if it means closing down Washington."

"Maybe the shark will swim away," the President said hopefully. "To Virginia."

"We're taking a terrible chance. We have to warn Congress that they can't go skinny-dipping in the Reflecting Pool."

"I don't see why," the President said. "They haven't passed one bill I've asked them to. I don't owe them anything."

"But as President it's your job to alert the country when a shark is in its territorial waters," the aide argued.

"I think we should give it another week or two," the President said. "If the shark eats another congressman, I'll close down the pool."

"That will be too late. The Democrats will charge you with being soft on sharks in 1976. You've got to take some kind of action now."

"Oh, all right. Nelson, how about setting up a National Shark Commission to investigate any illegal domestic acts by sharks in the United States? I want a full report in six months, and this time, Nelson, let *me* announce the results for a change."

"Yes, sir, Mr. President."

"Well, that should take care of the matter," the President said. "And let's keep this quiet. We don't want to spoil Congress' summer."

How to Succeed in Business

HELP WANTED

One of the toughest jobs in the country today is to be a personnel officer for a company doing business with the government.

Everett Dollop, a friend who hires people for Ozone Aviation, was telling me his troubles the other night.

"I'm going crazy," he said. "The law says that when a federal contract is awarded to a company, the employer is required to draw up an 'affirmative action plan' for hiring, which means he has to show he will hire minorities and women appropriate to the general skills."

"What's wrong with that?" I asked.

"Nothing except that the law also states that firms with government contracts have to submit reports to the government on how many veterans they've hired."

"So?"

"So," said Dollop, "we eliminate male whites over twenty-five years of age to start with."

"Why over twenty-five years of age?"

"Because there is a federally supported program to promote the hiring of youths and we're pledged to support it."

"So when it comes to a job," I said, "you have your choice of women, minorities, veterans, and youths."

"And handicapped people. The law requires employers

Bob threw his racket down in disgust and walked off the court.

It went on like this for months. Then rumors started flying. Bob was sneaking off to volley with a Virginia Slims cigarette girl at the McLean Indoor Tennis Courts. Patty took to secretly lobbing in the morning and picking up any strange man to play with her.

It came as no surprise when Patty finally flew off to Wimbledon to get a divorce.

She charged Bob with incompatibility.

He charged her with foot faulting.

He also said she always called his baseline shots out.

She said he never gave her enough money for new tennis balls.

He said she squandered the household money on gut instead of nylon tennis strings.

The judge decided there were enough grounds for a divorce. He awarded Patty the Gucci tennis bag but gave Bob visiting right to see his trophies.

Bob and Patty rarely see each other anymore, but when they do, they walk on opposite sides of the net.

The members of the Racquet Club are split down the middle on the breakup. The wives think Patty was to blame for never developing a spin on her serve. But the husbands all say, "Bob was at fault. He shouldn't have encouraged Patty to play tennis in the first place."

Is There an Energy Crisis?

SABER RATTLING IN WASHINGTON

There is a certain amount of saber rattling going on in Washington. Henry Kissinger in a *Business Week* interview did not rule out the use of force against oil-producing nations if they strangled the West. It is one thing to make such threats but another to carry them out.

The major problem for the United States seems to be that, in order to pay for foreign oil, we've been exporting all sorts of military equipment to the very countries that we're saber rattling against.

There must be some wild meetings going on at the Pentagon these days.

An assistant secretary for defense says, "I'm happy to report that we've sold five billion dollars' worth of F-14 jets to Iran."

An Air Force general says, "But we were promised the next batch of F-14 jets."

"I'm sorry," the assistant secretary of defense replies, "but we need the money from Iran so we can go into production on our new T-65 tanks, which we've sold to Saudi Arabia."

An Army general says, "What are we doing selling T-65 tanks to Saudi Arabia when our own armored units have been stripped bare to supply Israel?"

"Can you pay cash for the tanks?" the assistant secretary asks.

"You know I can't," the Army general says.

"Well, Saudi Arabia can. And if we're going to have a strong defense posture, we can't afford to just give away our tanks to the U.S. Army."

"Mr. Secretary, is there any word about my nuclear aircraft carrier?" an admiral asks.

"I have good news for you on that. You get the second one we're going to build."

"The second one? Who gets the first one?"

"Kuwait."

"Why is Kuwait getting a nuclear carrier before the U.S. Navy?"

"Because we couldn't afford to build it unless we sold a carrier to them. You see they're financing us on it, and it's only fair they get the prototype."

"Damn it," the admiral says. "What happens if the balloon goes up—and Kuwait has a nuclear carrier and we're still waiting for ours?"

"We'll just borrow some submarines from Libya," the assistant secretary says.

"This is ridiculous," the Air Force general says. "Everything we make we sell to our potential enemies."

"Well, it isn't my fault," the assistant secretary replies peevishly. "Military equipment costs money, and the only ones who seem to have any are the oil-producing countries. We can't afford to finance our defense unless they share in the cost of our new arms."

"Does this mean I'm not going to get any new helicopters?" the commandant of the Marine Corps asks.

"That decision hasn't been made yet. We did promise the sheikh of Abu Dhabi he'd get first crack at buying our helicopters. But he's now expressed an interest in antiaircraft missiles since we've sold the F-14s to Iran. If he doesn't want the helicopters, General, you can have them."

"Thank God he doesn't want antitank guns," the Army general says.

"He doesn't," the assistant secretary says, "but Qatar does."

"What the hell for?"

"To knock out the tanks we sold to Saudi Arabia."

WHERE ARE THEY NOW?

A few years ago everyone was hard at work vowing to conserve fuel. Americans had pledged themselves to finding new ways of saving energy and making the United States self-sufficient when it came to oil.

In the interests of finding out what has been done in the past, I did a personal "Where Are They Now?" research project.

This is what I found.

C. Carruthers Ringold, chairman of the board of General Chrysford, the largest manufacturer of automobiles, is still in Detroit pushing the sales of large cars.

When he was reminded he promised last fall that General Chrysford would devote its efforts to the production of small cars that would not consume so much gasoline, Ringold replied, "No one is going to tell us what kind of automobiles to make. The profits are in the large cars, and that's what the public wants. When America wants small cars, we'll make them. If it wasn't for the environmental nuts, there would be more than enough gasoline for everybody."

Alan K. Lomitil, who was one of the first organizers of car pooling in Fairfax County, Virginia, is now driving to work alone. "Car pooling is a drag," Alan told me. "Who wants to talk to four other guys every morning? I think a man's automobile is his castle, and there is no reason he should share it with anybody else."

Mrs. Helen Klinger, the principal of PS 145, said that

she no longer believed in keeping the thermostat in her school down at 68. "We froze our tushies off last year," she told me, "and we don't intend to do it again. Congress ought to investigate the oil and gas companies and find out where the heat is *really* going. Heaven knows the schools aren't getting any of it."

Gaylor Prather, the advertising account executive for Windfall of New Mexico Gasoline Company, is still turning out copy, but the conservation campaign has been abandoned: "Since our business is selling gasoline, it's counterproductive to ask people to use less of it. Sure, it didn't hurt to say we were worried about future fuel supplies and we were doing everything to see that America would never have to do without. But I'll tell you one thing, the campaign didn't sell a gallon of gas. If anything, it scared people and they didn't care what brand of gasoline they bought. So we said the hell with it—the company has to come first."

Congressman Gunther Zilch, who led the fight for energy conservation, is not sure whether he's for it now. "This is an election year," Zilch told me, "and it's hardly the time to ask people to make sacrifices. Heaven knows the voter has enough to worry about without asking him to give up the comforts of home and the road."

I went over to the Department of Transportation and spoke to one of the top officials. "You people said you were going to have a crash program in mass urban transportation so people would use buses and trains again instead of private cars. Are you still going ahead with it?" He replied, "Yes, we're doing a study on it right now and it should be ready by 1985."

Professor Heinrich Applebaum, who predicted that shale oil would solve all our problems for the next 500 years, now has doubts about it. "That stuff is really hard," Applebaum said. "I mean squeezing oil out of a rock is some stupid way of getting fuel. Anyone who thinks we're going to solve our energy problems with shale oil in the near future is off his rocker. I don't know why the press takes people like me seriously."

IS THERE AN ENERGY CRISIS?

The country becomes more and more divided every day on whether there is an energy crisis or not. Those who *can't* get gas say there is one—but those who *can* get gas say there isn't. Whom are we to believe? The following questions and answers may shed some light on the problem.

Q. If there is an energy crisis, why can we still get gasoline?

A. Because people *believe* there is a crisis, which there is not, at the moment. If people *didn't* believe there was a crisis, there would be one, because then they would avoid conserving fuel.

Q. You mean in order not to have an energy crisis, you have to believe there is one?

A. Exactly. The people who are angriest about the energy crisis are those who can get all the fuel they want. They believe if they can get oil, that means the crisis is a fraud. It's hard to make a man feel humble when he has a full tank of gas.

Q. Why was William Simon picked as energy czar?

A. Because of his name. All of us played Simon Says as children, and the president felt Americans instinctively would obey Simon or be eliminated from the game. Mr. Nixon realized very early in the crisis that no one would obey an energy czar if his name were Love.

Q. Why are the oil companies the only ones who know how much fuel there is available in the country?

A. Because they are the only ones who have nothing to gain by an oil shortage. If you can't trust an oil company during a crisis, whom can you trust?

Q. You hear a lot of talk about leakage in the oil industry. What is it?

A. Every pump in an Arab country leaks a certain amount of oil. This oil is soaked up with a sponge, wrung out in buckets, and sold to countries that the Arabs are mad at because of Israel.

Q. Then the Arab embargo on oil is not working?

A. You can't say that. If you did, the Arabs would have to make it work, and they are reluctant to do so. We know that they know that we know where the oil is coming from. But if we admit it, then they know that we know that they would have to do something about it. So everyone says the embargo is working to make certain that it doesn't work.

Q. What are the bright spots to come out of the energy crisis?

A. There are many more things than one can list. Airlines have been able to cut out unprofitable flights to towns they were supposed to service, companies can raise prices and put it all on the fuel shortage, landlords can cut heat and raise the rent, and all the polluters in the country can blame the energy crisis on the ecologists.

Q. Will there be gasoline rationing?

A. It depends on which night of the week you watch the news on television. On odd days government officials announce there will be no gas rationing. On even days they say there is a good chance there will be. Sundays they can go either way.

Q. How much will the oil-producing countries charge for their oil if there is a Middle East settlement of the war?

A. Fourteen dollars a barrel.

Q. How much will they charge if there is no settlement?

A. Fourteen dollars a barrel.

Q. What can I, Mr. Average Citizen, do to avert a gas shortage this summer?

A. Take a sheikh to lunch.

WHITE-COLLAR CRIME

Federal investigators are now looking into charges that at the height of the Arab oil embargo American businessmen overcharged electric power companies, hospitals, schools, and consumers by as much as a billion, possibly $3 billion.

I couldn't believe that Americans could do this to other Americans, and I went to see Rock Oglethorpe, the spokesman for the Our Country Right or Wrong Oil Institute.

"Rock," I said, "how could you rip off your own people during an oil crisis?"

Rock touched the American flag in his lapel nervously. "If we didn't, somebody else would have."

"But you took advantage of poor people who were dependent on electricity for heat and cooking: widows, orphans, schoolchildren, and sick patients. Doesn't that bother your conscience?"

"What about our stockholders?" Rock said defensively. "They certainly deserve a fair return on their investment. The price of oil is made in the marketplace. When the Arabs shut off their spigots, we had two choices: sell oil at the fixed prices the government laid down or make a few bucks for a rainy day. This whole thing is exaggerated. We are talking about a few pennies for the average consumer. Would you like to see what we're doing to attract fish around our ocean-going oil rigs?"

"No," I said. "I want to talk to you about some of your dealers forging tanker invoices so that they could charge ten dollars for five dollar-barrels of oil."

Rock was getting red in the face. "Now you're dealing with national security. The Russians would love to know how we did it, but you're never going to find out from me. The point is that the power companies in this country needed oil desperately, and thanks to the American free-enterprise system, we delivered that oil. Suppose we have another crisis? We're going to have to do the same thing again. If the Commies knew how we made windfall profits on the Arab oil embargo, we'd all be dead ducks. Think of your country, man, before you write this story."

"Rock, I've known you for years. You support the National Symphony, the Boy Scouts of America, the Metropolitan Opera, the church of your choice. Why do you have to cheat people on their electricity bills?"

"We didn't cheat anybody. All we did was sell oil to the electric companies. We didn't tell them what to charge their customers. If they raised their prices, it had nothing to do with us. We're not in the power business."

"Do you believe that the men involved in the schemes should be brought to justice?"

"Of course. If they did anything wrong, they should be fined two thousand dollars or three thousand dollars. After all, we don't condone crime."

"I wasn't thinking of a fine. I was thinking more of sending them to jail for maybe five or ten years or, since we're talking about a billion dollars, maybe twenty years."

Rock was shocked. "You don't send businessmen to jail just for overcharging people. After all, they have families and are pillars of their community. Let's keep this in perspective. Jail is for people who commit crime in the streets. If there was any hanky-panky, and I'm not saying there was, no one was taken to the hospital."

"I guess you're right, Rock. No one did get hurt."

"Let's forget all this talk," Rock said. "It depresses me.

Would you like to see a film on how oil companies are
saving the alligators in the Everglades?"

A NEW IMAGE FOR RIP-OFF

The Rip-off Oil company was worried. A meeting of the
executive committee was called at a Duck Shoot Club
in South Carolina to discuss ways and means of combating
the bad publicity petroleum companies were getting over
the energy crisis.

Harlan Mudbank, president of Rip-off, presented the
problem.

"Gentlemen, I am sorry to say that the oil companies
have a very bad image because of the fuel shortage that
unfortunately has gripped the country in the last six
months. The purpose of this meeting is to find a way to
tell our story to the American people. Are there any
suggestions?"

Wilton Willbank, the advertising vice-president, said,
"Why don't we launch a national advertising campaign to
show that in spite of the crisis, Rip-off is keeping its prices
down?"

"Excellent," said Mudbank, "but where do we get the
money to pay for the campaign?"

Willbank replied, "By raising the price of our gasoline
a penny a gallon."

Mudbank smiled. "Good thinking. If there are no objections, the proposal is accepted. Are there any other ideas?"

Marvin Snowbank, vice-president in charge of public
affairs, said, "It seems to me the key to a good image is
Congress. We must persuade our lawmakers that we are
doing the best we can to provide the necessary fuel at
reasonable cost to the consumer."

"How do we do this?"

Snowbank opened his folder. "By contributing to the
political campaigns of *everyone* running for office."

"But," said Mudbank, "that would cost us a fortune."

Snowbank read from a paper. "Our Washington lobbyists believe we can do it by adding only two cents to what we are now charging for a gallon of gas."

"It doesn't seem to be out of line," the comptroller said. "It cost us a cent a gallon just to elect Nixon. For two cents a gallon we're getting an entire Congress."

"Good," said Mudbank. "We seem to be making progress. What else can we do to win the hearts and minds of the American people?"

Rineholt Sandbank, the vice-president for finacial affairs, said, "One of the things that seems to be bugging the American people is our profit picture. I estimate we stand to make a hundred and sixty percent profit after taxes this year. We must persuade the country that these profits are within the cost-of-living guidelines."

"How?" Mudbank asked.

"By distributing American flag pins for every customer's lapel. I can't conceive of anyone questioning our profits if we give them a free American flag."

"Those lapel flags aren't cheap," the comptroller protested.

"Well, pass on the cost of them to the customer. Three cents a gallon is a small price to pay for the privilege of wearing Old Glory," said Sandbank.

No objection was raised, and Mudbank continued.

"While we're at it, I'd like to bring up another problem. No one is certain how long this energy crisis will last. There may come a day when new sources of energy will be found. It is even possible that someone will develop an automobile that doesn't use gasoline. In twenty years this could put us in a terrible profit squeeze. We can't wait until it happens. We must prepare for it now. What do we do?"

The vice-president for financial affairs said, "It's obvious. We charge an extra nickel a gallon which we'll invest in taxfree bonds. No one can object to our ensuring ourselves against future unfair competition."

Mudbank seemed very pleased. "This has been a most successful meeting. Now let's all go out and shoot some ducks."

MAKE A LIST

In his closing speech to the economic summit, President Ford told Americans to "make up a list of 10 ways you can save energy and fight inflation. Little things that have become habits, but that don't really affect your health and happiness. . . . Exchange your family's list with your neighbors—and send me a copy."

Dear Mr. President,

Enclosed please find my list of ways we could save energy and fight inflation. As soon as I made it, I went over to see my neighbor Schlumberger and asked him for his list. Schlumberger hadn't made up his yet, which didn't surprise me. It takes him three weeks to cut his lawn, and he still hasn't returned the lawn chairs he borrowed in June.

"Schlumberger," I said, "the President has asked us how we can save energy and fight inflation. My wife and I notice you always leave the light on in your bathroom. Now it's obvious to us that there isn't somebody in the bathroom *all* the time. Why couldn't you turn the light out when no one is there?"

Instead of Schlumberger accepting this in the spirit in which it was given, he said something like "We'll keep our"—and then he said a terrible word—"bathroom lights on all night long if we want to."

I then went to item No. 2. "I notice you always seem to drive to work alone. Is there any reason you can't car pool it?"

Well, Mr. President, I want you to know Schlumberger started screaming and yelling and telling me to mind my own (and then there was that word again) business. I couldn't believe someone would be so selfish during a crisis of this proportion.

I was tempted not to bring up item No. 3, but I decided the interests of the country came first, so I said, "It appears the fuel truck comes around to your house every two months. The oilman told my wife you keep your thermostat at seventy-four degrees. Why couldn't you close off a few rooms in the winter and turn the dial down to sixty-seven degrees?"

I want to tell you, Mr. President, you would have thought I asked Schlumberger to go streaking down Pennsylvania Avenue at high noon. He said he would keep the (put the word here) thermostat at any (the word again) temperature he (word) pleased. And then he said a strange thing. He said why didn't I worry about my own (word) thermostat?

I had a good mind to just walk out, but I still had a few more things on my list. "Schlumberger," I said, "that gaslight you have in front of your house—it seems to me it's just a habit with you. Does it really do anything to affect your health or happiness?"

I guess I touched a sore nerve because Schlumberger asked me to get out of his (I wish he had a larger vocabulary) house.

I know it comes as a shock to you, Mr. President, that there are such thin-skinned people in this country. I went to the next item on my list which was what Schlumberger was doing about inflation. I said, "My wife and I went through your garbage last night and we were shocked to see how much good food your family wastes and—"

Mr. President, I know you're not going to believe this, but Schlumberger grabbed me by the back of my coat and pants and pushed me right out the front steps. I almost broke my arm.

Anyway, here's the list you asked for. Maybe you can do more with Schlumberger than I can. As you can see from my account, he's not much for jawboning. He's really a first-class (use any word you want).

Sincerely,
ART BUCHWALD

PEDESTRIANS ARE BACK

The energy crisis is not all bad. One of the organizations that has benefited from it is the American Pedestrian Association, which is involved with protecting the rights of pedestrians.

Arch Threetoes, the president of APA, said 1978 could be their greatest year.

"The pedestrian is coming back," he said happily. "Our membership is up thirty percent, and if we have rationing, it could triple by summer. Every time someone runs out of gas you've created another pedestrian."

"It must be a great feeling to have made such great strides," I said.

"I wouldn't be human if I didn't gloat. For years people thought of a pedestrian as someone who couldn't afford a car. The entire economy was based on reducing the pedestrian population of the country. Those who couldn't be shamed into buying an automobile were run over to teach them a lesson. Drivers honked their horns at us in contempt to make us get out of the way. Anyone who walked to work was considered a nut. We had to breathe the foul air that automobiles produced, and any time we protested that sidewalks were being cut down to make more room for roads, we were told we were destroying America. We suffered for a long time, but now we're having our day."

"It must do your heart good to see those long lines in front of gas stations," I said.

"I feel warm all over," Threetoes admitted. "But at the same time pedestrians do not hold grudges. We're going to take back anyone who sincerely says he wants to walk again."

"It must be hard to get people to admit that," I said.

"They have to swallow a lot of pride. After all, drivers considered the pedestrian their number one enemy. To ease the blow, I've given orders to all members of the

American Pedestrian Association not to rub it in. When a man's gas tank is empty, he is in a very bad psychological state, and if someone taunts him about it, he could resort to violence."

"Having so many pedestrians back must cause tremendous problems for you."

"Our biggest problem is teaching people how to walk again. Most adult Americans have forgotten how, and children have never known. We have schools now where people can learn the rudiments of walking. It's actually quite simple, and most of them get the hang of it in a week. We've signed up entire families. Would you like to see one of our classes?"

I said I would, and Threetoes took me down to the first floor into a gymnasium. The instructor was standing in front of a class of about thirty people. Some men were carrying briefcases; several women were carrying shopping bags; a few children had schoolbooks.

The instructor barked, "All right, now let's try it once again. Put your left foot out. . . . Your left foot, dummies. . . . Now bring your right foot forward past your left in a straight line. . . ."

Half the class tripped and fell to the floor. Some were giggling, and others were red-faced. The instructor blew his whistle. "Dammit, didn't I tell you *not* to hit your left foot with your right foot when you brought it forward? Everybody on their feet. Let's try it again. I'm going to make pedestrians out of you if it kills me."

Threetoes whispered to me, "He's one of our best instructors. Only fifteen percent of his classes don't make it."

ARABIAN KNOW-HOW

By the 1980s, if the predictions come true, the Arab oil countries will have all the money in the world. They will have to invest this money, and it is not inconceivable that they could own most of the large corporations in the United States.

Like any businessmen, they will demand a good return on their money, and I can imagine a meeting of the president of the Abu Dhabi General Motors Corporation of America (ADGMCA), a subsidiary of the Abu Dhabi General Motors Corporation International, and the sheikh.

The president, a citizen of the United States, has been called back to Abu Dhabi to explain why profits have been off.

The sheikh is in an angry mood.

"I have just seen the figures for 1982. They're disgraceful. I am the laughingstock of the Middle East Stock Exchange. The Libyan Bell Telephone Company of America shows a ten percent increase in profits. The Saudi Arabian Coca-Cola Company of the United States is up fifteen percent, and the shah's Sears, Roebuck Corporation is predicting record earnings. What have you been doing over there?"

The president of ADGMCA is on his knees bowed in front of the sheikh. "Forgive me, sire. We thought we'd have a good year, but then you people imposed your one thousand eight hundred and ninety-sixth oil embargo and auto sales dropped."

"That wasn't my fault," the sheikh says. "The Standard Oil Company of Saudi Arabia has been putting the squeeze on gasoline. They think if they can cut down production, they can get twenty-five dollars a gallon for their gas. But if they don't watch it, they're going to get into a price war.

"I've ordered my Abu Dhabi Royal Shell Company to hold the line at twenty-three dollars a gallon. There is no sense driving people away from the pumps. But to get back to your problem. When I bought General Motors two years ago as a present for my wife, I said I wouldn't tinker with management as long as I could get a decent return on my investment. There were some people here who thought I should send over Abu Dhabi tribesmen to run the show. But I said we should give the American natives a chance to prove they could do it on their own. Obviously, I was wrong."

The president was still on his knees. "Please, sire, we expect a turnaround by the end of this year. The Kuwaiti Chrysler Corporation of America is also in great difficulty, and even the Yemen Ford Company of the United States has shown losses. Rumor has it that Yemen may fire its American manager, Henry Ford."

"I don't want excuses," the sheikh of Abu Dhabi yells. "I want results. Thank Allah I don't have to depend on General Motors for my main source of income. Do you know I make more money from the Abu Dhabi Consolidated Edison Company of New York than I do from GM? If you want the truth, I'm tempted to sell the American subsidiary of General Motors and buy the Chase Manhattan Bank instead."

"But that is owned by the sheikh of Bahrein," the president says.

"I think I can throw in the Prudential Life Insurance Company for it as well," the sheikh replies.

"Please, sire, give me another chance," the president begs. "If you dismiss me, there isn't an Arab company in America that will hire me. I'll get up production if I have to flog every autoworker personally. We'll cut off the left hand of any salesman who doesn't meet his quota. We'll hang by the thumbs the account executive of our advertising agency if the cars don't sell."

"All right," the sheikh says. "But if I don't get back twenty percent on my investment next year, I'm going to cover you with sand and pour honey on your head and let the red ants have a go at you."

"Bless you, sire. It's no wonder they call you the Howard Hughes of the Middle East."

6

Biting the Bullet

MAIL DAY

POST OFFICE THREATENS TO CUT DOWN DELIVERIES TO THREE TIMES A WEEK—headline in a recent newspaper.

It had to happen. In the year 1980 the postmaster general went on television and announced to the country that because of a $600 billion deficit and Congress' refusal to permit him to charge $5 for a first-class stamp, the American people would receive their mail only *one* day a year. This would be known as Mail Day and would be considered a national holiday. He regretted the decision but assured the American people that they would still receive the best service of any postal system in the world, and he assured everyone that with only a few exceptions no one would be inconvenienced by it.

At first people were angered by the news, but pretty soon they accepted it as they have everything else the U.S. Postal Service has done to them.

In a few years Mail Day became as popular as Christmas and the excitement built up as the day came near.

Little children were told that if they were bad the Mailman (he was pictured as a man in a blue uniform with a long white beard) wouldn't bring them any Records of the Month. Department stores hired men to play the role of Mailman, and men and women and children would sit on his knee and tell them what they wanted for Mail Day.

People decorated their doors and windows with old birthday and get well cards and put colored lights on their mailboxes.

The hit record played for weeks before Mail Day was Bing Crosby's rendition of "I'm Dreaming of a Sears, Roebuck Catalogue." There was a great spirit of goodwill associated with the holiday. Doormen and elevator operators and building superintendents became kinder and more attentive. People greeted each other by saying, "Have a Merry Mail Day." Charity organizations raised funds on the streets for poor people who had no one to share their mail with.

Fraternal groups got together and walked through the streets singing Mail Carols. The churches and synagogues stayed open on Mail Day Eve so people could pray for letters from their children.

When youngsters asked where the mailman lived, their parents told them he lived at the North Pole and he spent the entire year canceling stamps on letters and packages so he could leave them on Mail Day morning for them. When they asked how he delivered the mail, they were told he put it in bags and came down the chimney when everyone was sleeping. But if there were a dog in the house, he would pass it by. Everyone locked up their dogs on Mail Day Eve.

On the morning of Mail Day the entire family came downstairs and opened their bags of mail. Mothers got all the bills; fathers got all the newspapers and magazines that had piled up for the year. There were letters and postcards and birthday cards for everyone. Grandmothers and grandfathers opened their Social Security checks. Children gleefully ripped open the junk mail with four-color catalogues and appeals from Indian reservations that didn't exist. There were also packages from stores and mail-order houses and tax returns and alumni fund appeals.

It took all day for people to open the mail. In the evening relatives came by to exchange canceled stamps and have Mail Day dinner with each other. Every TV network put on a televised football game, and Andy Williams had a special Mail Day TV program with his entire family.

For ten years Mail Day was the most exciting day of the year. But then in January, 1990, the postmaster general appeared on television and said that because of rising costs and a $2 trillion deficit the post office would be unable to deliver mail once a year as it had done in the past.

In the future, he said, mail would be delivered only one day during leap year. He felt that in this way the post office could operate with more efficiency and still provide the services that so many people depend on. But he warned that if Congress did not raise the price of a first-class stamp to $49 a letter, the post office would have to take more drastic measures, which included only delivering the mail once every bicentennial year.

ECONOMICS MADE EASY

I listened to the economic summit for two days and it was a great inspiration to see so many learned men from all walks of life tell us why the country is in such a mess. Although there was some disagreement, this is what we now know for sure.

The Republicans are responsible for inflation because of their tight money policies, high interest rates, and giving in to big business at every turn.

The Democrats are responsible for inflation because of their large welfare programs, reckless government spending, and catering to the interests of labor.

In order to cure the upward spiral of prices, we have to make more money available for business investment.

We must make bank loans more difficult for business investment.

Arthur Burns of the Federal Reserve Board is responsible for the recession we are in.

George Meany is responsible for the recession we're in.

There is no recession.

We cannot solve our economic problems until we bring down the cost of fuel, particularly oil and natural gas.

The only way we can get more fuel is to raise the price of oil and gas to encourage the oil companies.

Congress is responsible for the crisis because of the large amounts of money it has voted for unneeded government programs.

Congress has to vote new funds to keep the country from going into a depression.

Unless we have a tax cut, the economy will never recover from the doldrums it is in.

The only way to lick inflation is to raise taxes and keep the dollar from being devalued.

The Arabs are responsible for all our troubles.

There is no inflation. Our main problem is stagflation.

We must stop selling agricultural products abroad so we can bring down the price of food at home.

We must increase our food exports so we can have a more favorable balance of payments.

Labor has to show more responsibility when asking for wage increases.

Labor is being penalized for the mistakes of management.

We must have wage and price controls to ward off disaster.

Introduction of wage and price controls would be a disaster.

The people who are suffering the most from inflation are the poor, the sick, and the old.

The people who are suffering the most from inflation are the brokers.

We cannot lick inflation overnight.

Inflation must be licked overnight.

Summit conferences are the best way to resolve differences in economic philosophies.

Calling back Nixon's economists to tell us how we can win the battle against inflation is like asking the Italian general staff to tell us how to win World War II.

HOW THE RECESSION HAPPENED

The recession hit so fast that nobody knows exactly how it happened. One day we were the land of milk and honey, and the next day we were the land of sour cream and food stamps.

This is one explanation.

Hofberger, the Chevy salesman in Tomcat, Virginia, a suburb of Washington, called up Littleton, of Littleton Menswear & Haberdashery, and said, "Good news, the new Impalas have just come in, and I've put one aside for you and your wife."

Littleton said, "I can't, Hofberger. My wife and I are getting a divorce."

Hofberger said, "That's too bad. Then take the car for yourself. I'll give you a hundred dollars extra on a trade-in because of the divorce."

"I'm sorry," Littleton said, "but I can't afford a new car this year. After I settle with my wife, I'll be lucky to buy a bicycle."

Hofberger hung up. His phone rang a few minutes later.

"This is Bedcheck, the painter," the voice on the other end said. "When do you want us to start painting your house?"

"I changed my mind," said Hofberger. "I'm not going to paint the house."

"But I ordered the paint," Bedcheck said. "Why did you change your mind?"

"Because Littleton is getting a divorce and he can't afford a new car."

That evening, when Bedcheck came home, his wife said, "The new color television set arrived from Gladstone's TV Shop."

"Take it back," Bedcheck told his wife.

"Why?" she demanded.

"Because Hofberger isn't going to have his house painted now that the Littletons are getting a divorce."

The next day Mrs. Bedcheck dragged the TV set in its carton back to Gladstone. "We don't want it."

Gladstone's face dropped. He immediately called his travel agent, Sandstorm. "You know that trip you had scheduled for me to the Virgin Islands?"

"Right, the tickets are all written up."

"Cancel it. I can't go. Bedcheck just sent back the color TV set because Hofberger didn't sell a car to Littleton because they're going to get a divorce and she wants all his money."

Sandstorm tore up the airline tickets and went over to see his banker, Gripsholm. "I can't pay back the loan this month because Gladstone isn't going to the Virgin Islands."

Gripsholm was furious. When Rudemaker came in to borrow money for a new kitchen he needed for his restaurant, Gripsholm turned him down cold. "How can I lend you money when Sandstorm hasn't repaid the money he borrowed?"

Rudemaker called up the contractor, Eagleton, and said he couldn't put in a new kitchen. Eagleton laid off eight men.

Meanwhile, General Motors announced it was giving a rebate on its new models. Hofberger called up Littleton immediately. "Good news," he said. "Even if you are getting a divorce, you can afford a new car."

"I'm not getting a divorce," Littleton said. "It was all a misunderstanding, and we've made up."

"That's great," Hofberger said. "Now you can buy the Impala."

"No way," said Littleton. "My business has been so lousy I don't know why I keep the doors open."

"I didn't know that," Hofberger said.

"Do you realize I haven't seen Bedcheck, Gladstone, Sandstorm, Gripsholm, Rudemaker, or Eagleton for more than a month? How can I stay in business if they don't patronize my store?"

BITING THE BULLET

When President Ford said we all have to bite the bullet on the economy, I immediately went down to my local sporting goods store.

"I would like a bullet, please," I said to the clerk.

"You mean a box of bullets," he corrected me.

"No, just one would be enough."

He looked at me suspiciously. "What kind of bullet do you want?"

"I don't know. Are there different kinds?"

"Of course. What kind of gun do you have?" he asked.

"I don't have a gun," I said.

"Then what do you want a bullet for?"

"I want to bite it," I admitted sheepishly.

The clerk backed away from me, trying to reach a buzzer which I assumed turned on some kind of alarm.

"Don't get frightened," I said. "You see, Jerry Ford, as part of his economic message, said that every one of us has to bite the bullet or we'll never lick it."

"The bullet?" he asked.

"No, inflation, dummy," I said.

"And he didn't say what caliber of bullet he wanted Americans to bite?"

"Not that I know of," I replied. "Does it make a difference?"

"I would think so," the clerk said. "I mean people have different size mouths, and what might be comfortable for you might not necessarily be comfortable for your grocer. Here, try this twenty-two bullet."

He placed it in my mouth. I bit on it.

"How does that feel?" he asked.

"Not too bad. How does it look?"

"You have the shell casing sticking out. Did the President indicate what part of the bullet he wanted you to bite?"

"Come to think of it, he didn't," I said. "The least Mr. Ford could have done is tell us which end of the bullet we should get our teeth into."

"Maybe he thought everyone in the United States had bitten a bullet before," the clerk suggested.

"He shouldn't take those things for granted," I said. "Listen, my teeth are starting to hurt. You don't have another kind, do you?"

"We have a soft-nosed lead thirty-eight dumdum, but they're illegal to shoot."

"Are they illegal to bite?"

"I'll have to check that out." The clerk called his superior upstairs. Then he hung up. "My boss said to the best of his knowledge, there is no law against biting a lead bullet as long as you don't spit it out at somebody afterward."

I put it in my mouth.

"It's more comfortable than the twenty-two," I said. "And it has a nice taste to it."

"Would you like to try a forty-five?" the clerk asked. "It's thicker than a thirty-eight and lasts twice as long."

"No, I think the thirty-eight bullet will do nicely. How much is it?"

"Let's see," the clerk said. "On the box it says the bullets are four cents each. But we just got a bulletin from the manufacturer telling us they now cost eight cents. Since this was mailed out *last* week, we have to assume the cost went up another two cents. But we don't know what will happen *next* week, do we?"

I admitted we didn't.

"We'd better add another four cents on the bullet just to be safe. Therefore, it will cost you fourteen cents."

"That's outrageous!" I said.

The clerk shrugged his shoulders as he wrote out the sales slip. "Maybe if you bite on it long enough, the price will go down."

A SOCIAL DISEASE

"The worst part of being unemployed," said Kellerman, "outside of the fact you have no money, is the social stigma attached to it. Americans get very nervous when they talk to somebody who doesn't have a job."

"I hadn't thought about it, but I believe you're right. Why is that?"

"We're a country who likes to put everyone into a slot. The first question anyone asks you after he meets you is 'What do you do?' or 'What does your husband do?' or 'What does your father do?' People want to be sure they're talking to somebody respectable."

"Why can't you just say you're a salesman?"

"Because the second question is 'Whom do you work for?' They're not just going to let you off the hook by accepting the fact that you're a salesman."

"And that's the crunch? Because then you have to admit you don't have a job."

"Right. People tend to be sympathetic, but you start to feel bad vibrations, as if you've just told them you have a social disease. They begin looking for a chance to move away."

"That's terrible."

"We're prisoners of our own work ethic. We've been told for such a long time that the only people in this country who are unemployed are those who are lazy, shiftless, and don't give a damn. In America, not having a job makes you an outcast, except for the kids, of course, who really don't care who is working and who isn't."

"They have a healthier attitude."

"It isn't just friends," Kellerman said. "It's relatives as well. They get nervous for a different reason. They're afraid that if you don't have a job it's going to cost them money. I used to see my brother-in-law two, three times a week. Since I've been out of work, he's suddenly found himself the busiest guy in Maryland. I don't want anything from him, but I guess he feels he should offer to help us out, and since he obviously doesn't want to, the best thing is not to see me.

"The sad thing is now that I'm out of work I have time on my hands to see friends and do things, but no one wants to see me. The only people who are really friendly are those you meet while you're standing in the unemployment lines. It may be my imagination, but they seem much nicer than people who are working."

"They probably are. But perhaps people's attitudes toward the unemployed are based on fear. Maybe they're afraid your unemployment will rub off on them," I suggested.

"You're right. Americans haven't learned how to deal with a person who isn't working. Of course it's changing. There may be more of *us* than there are of *them* soon."

"I wish you hadn't said that," I muttered, starting to move away.

"You too?" Kellerman said.

"Heck, no, Kellerman. You know it doesn't matter whether you're working or not. I still look at you as I always have."

"You want to play tennis this afternoon?"

"Sure, but only on one condition. You let me pay for the balls."

"Forget it," he said sadly. "You've never paid for a can of balls in your life."

MONOPOLY, 1975

The family was playing Monopoly the other night and in the middle of the game, to make it more exciting, I suggested we update the rules according to 1975 economic conditions.

No one was sure this was a good idea until I, as banker, offered to give each player an extra $200 to encourage him to spend more money on his properties.

They thought this was great. But then I said, "In order to pay for this, I will have to charge you all double if you land on the Electric Company or the Waterworks which I happen to own."

There were screams of protest from everyone. "What good is the two hundred dollars if we have to give it back to you for electricity and water?" my daughter wanted to know.

"It will put more money into circulation and stimulate the buying of houses and hotels. I suggest that if you raise the rents on your properties by fifty percent, it will cover the cost of landing on the Electric Company. When I land on one of your properties, you'll get the money back."

"That's true," said my wife, "if you own Park Place or Boardwalk. But I own Baltic and Mediterranean Avenues. If I have to pay you double when I land on the Electric Company or the Waterworks, I'll be wiped out."

"You can always sell your property," I pointed out.

"Have you ever known anyone who wanted to buy Baltic and Mediterranean Avenues?" she asked bitterly.

"Well, we can't all live in Marvin Gardens," I retorted.

"There would be no Monopoly game if everyone could afford everything on the board. Now let's start playing."

My son landed on Go to Jail. He didn't have the two hundred dollars to get out, so I suggested he turn state's evidence.

"Against whom?" he asked.

"Against any of the other players. If you're willing to tell the district attorney what you know about what happened on Pennsylvania Avenue, I'll let you out on the next roll."

"That's unfair," my daughter said. "I had to stay in jail three turns because I didn't have the money to get out."

"Well, these are 1975 rules," I said. "And anyone who implicates someone else in a crime does not have to stay in jail."

"Okay," my son said. "Connie gave me a hundred dollars under the table so I would sell her North Carolina Avenue and she would have a monopoly on that property."

"You're a rat," Connie shouted. "You said you would give me North Carolina Avenue if I sold you St. Charles Place."

"Let's not fight," I said. "Joel, for telling all, I give you a pardon. Now it's your mother's turn to roll."

My wife nervously rolled the dice. She had to move her shoe token to Indiana Avenue which I owned. It had a hotel on it. "With the surcharge of fifty percent," I announced, "you owe me one thousand five hundred and seventy-five dollars rent."

"I don't have it," she said.

"I'll take Oriental, Vermont and Connecticut Avenues and all your money instead," I said.

"But then I would have nothing left but Baltic and Mediterranean Avenues," she protested. "I'll have to go on welfare."

"I'm not concerned with your problems," I replied.

"Hotels cost money, and besides, I'm thinking of putting up several houses on New York Avenue, Tennessee Avenue and St. James Place, in the high-rent district."

"Could I get a loan?" she asked.

"In your financial condition?" I hooted. "What kind of banker do you take me for?"

With all my property and money in front of me I rolled the dice next and moved my top-hat token to Community Chest. I picked up the top card and read out loud, "Income Tax Refund—Collect twenty dollars."

My wife, who had lost all her property and had three dollars left, said in disgust, "It figures."

"DID YOU HEAR THE ONE ABOUT . . . ?"

Professor Alan Greenspan, chief presidential economic adviser, endeared himself last week to the country with a remark he made to a group of leaders representing the old, sick, and handicapped. Greenspan said Wall Street stock brokers have suffered the most from the nation's economic decline.

When I saw Professor Greenspan say this deadpan on television, I broke into laughter and thought to myself, *The Ford administration does have humor after all.*

A few minutes later I received a call from a congressman friend asking me if I had written the line for Greenspan.

"I wish I had," I said. "It has to be one of the funniest things I've ever seen on television."

"Well, could you find out who his writer is? I need some jokes for my campaign this fall, and if Greenspan's man can come up with any other one-liners as good as this one, I'll be in clover."

I called the Council of Economic Advisers and spoke to a man on the phone.

"I'm trying to find out who Professor Greenspan's gag writer is."

"What are you talking about?" the man said.

"You know, the guy who wrote that line about Wall Street brokers hurting the most from inflation." I started laughing again as I said it.

The man on the other line said frostily, "Professor Greenspan meant every word he said. Brokers have suffered the most."

I was laughing so hard I couldn't stop. "I didn't think you economists went in for that kind of humor," I said. "Gosh, that's funny. Do you have any good ones?"

"You apparently believe that Professor Greenspan was joshing at his meeting with the representatives of the old, sick, and handicapped. But inflation is no joking matter. The professor was talking in terms of percentages. Whether the old, the sick, and the handicapped want to believe it or not, we have statistics to prove that brokers have been hit the hardest."

"Don't go too fast," I said, trying to contain myself. "I want to write this all down."

"You must remember that when inflation strikes, brokers' commissions, which are fixed by law, are immediately affected. When you have low turnover in Wall Street stocks, the broker is the first one to feel it. Who's hurt by high interest rates more than anybody else?"

"Don't tell me," I said, chuckling. "Let me guess."

"I'm not sure you're taking me seriously," the man said.

"Of course I am. I think the most important thing during a crisis is for people to laugh at themselves. If Professor Greenspan can provide us with a line like he did about the brokers every week, we can win the war against inflation. Let me ask you something. Does Greenspan have any good ones about people suffering in the oil industry?"

The man hung up on me.

I called back my friend in Congress. "I know you're not going to believe this," I said, "but Greenspan writes his own jokes."

"I'll be damned," said my friend. "You mean the line about the brokers was his?"

"Yup. Greenspan's a fountain of mirth, and he comes up with things like that all the time. It must be great for the President to have somebody like that around to take his mind off the economy."

THAT'S GOOD—THAT'S BAD

Everywhere I travel in this great land I am asked the same question about the economy: "Why doesn't the government do something?" The answer, as everyone in Washington knows, is that the government doesn't know what to do.

I was talking to my friend Baradash, a high government official, the other day.

"The price of meat should go down next month," he said.

"That's good."

"No, that's bad. If meat goes down, the cattlemen are going to get sore and shoot their calves. You see, they're paying more for everything and getting less for what they sell."

"That's bad," I said.

"It could be good if we could hold the line on meat so wages in other industries would not go up. The real problem is fertilizer. There's a shortage of fertilizer because there is a shortage of oil. Of course, Saudi Arabia and the United Arab Emirates cut the price of their oil last week."

"That's good."

"Not really. At the same time they cut the price of oil

they raised taxes on the oil companies, and it may cost us more for oil now than it did before."

"That's bad."

"And then we can't forget the coal strike in this country, can we?"

"You're really a joy to talk to, Baradash."

"Things aren't all that bad," he said. "Interest rates are going down."

"That's good." I brightened up.

"It won't solve our inflation problem, though. If money is easier to get, prices will probably go up again."

"That's bad."

"The important thing is that this country has been consuming too much. We've got to get people to conserve and not spend as if there were no tomorrow."

"It would be a good thing if they did," I agreed.

"It also could be a bad thing. If Americans don't spend as if there were no tomorrow, people will lose their jobs, and then they won't be able to buy new automobiles. If we don't sell any automobiles in this country, we're going to have a real recession, and then we'll have to raise taxes to take care of all the people who are out of work."

"That's bad."

"It could be good if we taxed gasoline because that would be the best way to cut down on our oil imports. If we could cut down on oil imports, we could have a better chance for a favorable balance of trade."

"That would be good," I said.

"It would be, but no one has any money to buy our exports, except possibly food. If we export our food, prices in the supermarkets will go soaring and we'll have a revolution at home."

"Baradash, you represent the government. Isn't there anything you people can do to stave off disaster?"

"Well, I'm wearing my WIN button, aren't I?" he said.

"That's good," I said.

"No," he replied. "That's bad. The damn thing cost me a buck, and it keeps making holes in my suits."

THE TOWERING INFERNO

The building was on fire and had been for a while. By the time the fire department arrived flames were pouring out the windows. Fire Chief Jerry Ford drove up, sirens screaming. He got out of his car and was immediately surrounded by his advisers.

"What do you think I ought to do?" he said.

"You've got to pour water on the fire to put it out."

"That's a good idea," he agreed.

"Wait," said another adviser. "If we pour too much water on the fire, the building will collapse."

"Good point," Chief Ford said.

"I think," said another adviser, "the first thing we have to do is save the people."

"No," another adviser said. "We have to save the building."

"We can always build another building," an adviser protested. "Let's get the people out."

"Foam would be better than water," another adviser yelled.

"Foam is too expensive," someone else said. "We've always put out fires with water before, and we will do it again."

"But this fire isn't like any other fire we've ever fought."

"I think we should let it go a little while longer," a lieutenant suggested. "It could burn itself out."

"A tough fire takes tough measures, Chief. Let's go."

"I like to hear everyone's opinion," Chief Ford said. "Try to draw up a plan in which we could save both the people and the building."

As the chief's lieutenants worked out different plans on the hood of the car, sirens were heard in the distance.

"What's that?" the chief asked.

"That's the ninety-fourth Democratic Congressional Fire Brigade. We need them to put out the fire."

The congressional fire brigade roared up and jumped off the trucks. They all stared at the building and shook their heads.

Chief Ford stood on the top of a hook and ladder.

"Men, the state of this building is bad. I don't want any applause."

There was none.

"I am determined to put this fire out, but I need your help. Now here is my plan."

"It stinks," a fireman shouted.

"An outrage," another fireman shouted.

"Wait a minute. You haven't heard it yet," the chief said.

"This is our plan," a fireman said. "We will save the people and put out the fire."

"But that's my plan," the fire chief protested.

"Yeah, but we know how to do it," the fireman said. "We have to put a lot of water on the building."

"That costs money, and I may need some water for another fire," Chief Ford said.

"Don't worry about other fires. Get this one out," the members of the fire brigade shouted.

The fire chief said, "I'm sure we can work something out so that your plan for fighting the conflagration will coincide with my plan. I'm willing to make some adjustments."

"We'll have to meet on that," the fire brigade said.

They all stood around the hook and ladders, arguing about how to put out the fire. Meanwhile, the chief went back to his car to work on a different plan.

As all this was taking place, the flames from the towering inferno kept licking away, and high over all the firemen and equipment in the street could be heard the piercing cries of the trapped people shouting, "H-E-LLLLLLLLLLPPPPPP!"

THE GUILTY ONES OF 1975

Who was to blame for what went wrong in 1975? There are a lot of theories by a lot of different people. I didn't talk to any of them, but this is what they probably would have told me.

President Ford: "Congress is responsible for everything that went wrong in 1975, and I want all the American people to know it."

Congress: "The Ford administration is responsible for all our troubles. Every time we passed legislation to help the country, the President vetoed it."

Ronald Reagan: "Both Ford and Congress must take full blame for the reckless spending in welfare, Social Security, and giveaway programs that this great country cannot afford."

Howard Cosell: "The Saturday night television audience who don't even know a good live show when they see one."

Cher: "Sonny."

Sonny: "Cher."

Nelson Rockefeller: "Hi, fella. I sure enjoyed 1975, and Happy and I couldn't be happier the way things turned out."

The oil companies: "The people to blame for 1975 are those who refused to let us raise prices and deregulate gas so that we could search for oil and provide this country with the energy sources it so desperately needs."

The bakery industry: "Earl Butz, for sending all that wheat to Russia."

Secretary of the Treasury William Simon: "All our troubles in 1975 can be traced to the fiscal irresponsibility of New York City."

New York City Mayor Abe Beame: "I have no one to blame but myself."

Patty Hearst: "I blame the San Francisco Police Department and the FBI who had nothing better to do than to hassle urban guerrillas."

The Listerine Mouthwash Company: "The FTC, that doesn't even care if people catch colds or not."

Squeaky Fromme: "The people who are trying to kill all the redwoods in California."

Richard Nixon: "I don't blame anyone. After all, the rats who drove me from office have a right to their opinion, and I would be the last one to say the lying media and my political enemies are to blame for what happened to me this year. I think history should judge how shabbily everyone treated me in 1975 after I was driven from office because I wanted to do what was right for America."

The CIA: "The American people, who are not willing to accept the fact we live in a dirty world and you have to use despicable, repugnant, and illegal methods to protect everyone's constitutional rights."

The FBI: "Whoever is responsible for what happened in 1975 is either dead or retired. We are asking for guidelines so we won't do the same thing in 1976."

Ralph Nader: "The EPA, the FTC, the FDA, HEW, the FCC, EEOC, AEC, the LEA, NIH, NIMH, NAM, OBM, YMCA, YWCA, A&P, ETC. ETC. ETC. ETC. ETC. ETC."

Henry Kissinger: "I am not responsible for anything that went wrong in 1975."

RECYCLING OIL MONEY

PARIS—"There's your problem," said François as an Arab sheikh walked by the bar at the Hôtel George V.

We were talking about the economy in Europe, and François was trying to explain it to me.

"You mean there are too many Arab sheikhs?" I asked him.

"No, I mean there are not enough sheikhs—oil sheikhs to be specific. This shortage of Arab potentates is killing everyone."

"How's that?"

"It's called recycling. When you Americans once had money, you came by the millions to Europe and spent it here. When you ran out of money and the Japanese had it all, they came here to spend it. We always complained about tourists, but it was one of the best ways to keep the money in circulation.

"Now," said François sadly, "the Arabs have all the money, and there are not enough of them to spread it around."

"I thought there were a lot of Arabs in the world," I said.

"There are," replied François, "but they are not the right kind. Only a few of them have any of the oil money. The king of Saudi Arabia, for example, who must have made twenty-one billion dollars on oil this year, has about one hundred and thirty-two sons and nephews. That means each son or nephew would have to spend one hundred and sixty million dollars for the rest of us to get even."

"That would be tough to do," I admitted.

"Most of the oil sheikhs leave their wives at home, so you don't get any business at Dior, Balenciaga or Givenchy. They don't buy any art, and they're not known for their wine consumption. What can they spend their money on?"

"Postcards?"

"Exactly. Even if they ate at Maxim's twice a day, they wouldn't be able to use up all the money that's rolling in. The other oil sheikhdoms are no better. I would say at the maximum there are about one thousand

Arab families who are responsible for recycling forty billion dollars a year. There is no way they can do it."

"What's the answer, François?"

"The oil kingdoms have to produce more Arabs. We have to start a population explosion program in Saudi Arabia, Abu Dhabi, Bahrain, and Kuwait so the royal families will give birth to more princes."

"Won't that take time?" I asked.

"Maybe, but if they start now, at least we'll have a change in the eighties when our oil bill will be somewhere around one hundred billion dollars."

"How do you persuade the Arab sheikhs to have more children?" I asked François.

"You give them free 'birth explosion' pills. You set up an Unplanned Parenthood Agency where you counsel them on the joys of having very large families. You persuade the sheikhs that the more mouths they have to feed, the easier it will be for them to get rid of their money."

"It sounds like a dream to me, François."

"Perhaps," he replied, "but if it works, I can see the day when there will be nothing but Arab princes walking down the Champs-Élysées. The Place de la Concorde will be filled with Cadillacs, the Folies Bergère will be jammed with burnooses, and there will be so many sheikhs in Paris that Frenchmen will scrawl in chalk on their walls, 'ARABIANS GO HOME!' "

The Arab sheikh came into the bar with three body-guards. They ordered Coca-Colas.

François whispered to me, "You see what I mean? How can you recycle a twenty-one-billion-dollar oil bill when all they buy is four Coca-Colas?"

7

Can This Marriage Be Saved?

AN AUGUST BRIEFING

Whenever I go away on vacation I have to get briefed when I get back to Washington on what I missed. The man I depend on to catch me up on things is Doc Dalinsky, my pharmacist, who keeps up on the news when he unstacks the papers every morning.

"What happened while I was gone?" I asked him.

"We sold ten million tons of grain to the Russians, which means the price of bread is going up in this country this year."

"Oh!" I exclaimed.

"It was a big mistake," Dalinsky told me.

"How's that?"

"Well, the original idea was to sell the Soviets ten million tons of New York City bonds. But somebody in Washington got his signals mixed and sold them the grain instead."

"Why would the Soviets want New York City bonds?"

"Because several of the banks in New York said that if the city couldn't sell them, someone would have to eat them. It was Mayor Beame's hope that the Russians would rather eat his bonds than somebody else's wheat."

"But it didn't work out that way?"

"No. The Soviets insisted they wanted grain, so New Yorkers have to eat their own bonds for breakfast."

"What else happened?" I asked Dalinsky.

"Let's see. Oh, yes. The United States is ending its trade curbs against Castro, and we'll probably recognize Cuba soon."

"That's a switch," I said.

"Well, the thinking is that after trying to knock Castro off twenty-four times and failing, the only thing left to do was open diplomatic relations with him."

"How does the Mafia feel about it?" I asked Dalinsky.

"They were kind of hurt that they weren't consulted, but I must say they were magnanimous about it. One of the heads of the families said, 'We have a saying in the Cosa Nostra: If you can't kill 'em, join 'em.' "

"What else is going on?"

"Kissinger's in the Middle East," Dalinsky said.

"That's not news," I said.

"The price of gasoline is going up."

"That's not news."

"We're going back to double-digit inflation."

"That's not news."

"Nixon said he did nothing wrong."

"That's not news."

"Liz Taylor and Richard Burton are back together again."

"That's not news," I said.

"Yes, it is. Because this time they say it's forever."

"Forever?"

"That's what their press spokesman said."

"What a story! They really said forever?"

"I'm not making it up," Dalinsky said.

"Is there anything else I should know?"

"Well, are you sitting down?"

"How can I be sitting down? I'm standing here talking to you."

"All right. Betty Ford revealed to Myra McPherson in *McCall's* magazine that she and her husband have given up the White House tradition of separate bedrooms for the President and his wife."

I whistled, "That's news."

"And she said if anyone ever asked her how often she slept with her husband, she would say, 'As often as possible.' "

"Damn," I said. "I knew I shouldn't have gone on vacation."

CAN THIS MARRIAGE BE SAVED?

As if Washington did not have enough to worry about, it now, for the umpteenth time, is sweating out consummation of the marriage between its two pet pandas, Hsing-Hsing and Ling-Ling. Everyone knows that those of us who live in the capital are a long-suffering people, but we're all losing patience with Hsing-Hsing, who either doesn't know, or doesn't care, about fulfilling his role as a husband and a father.

Zoo officials have indicated that Ling-Ling has been not only ready but eager to have a baby panda. But she has been unable to get Hsing-Hsing into the hay.

The people in this town are so upset about this state of affairs that they have raised a fund to hire a sex therapist to see if he could do something about Hsing-Hsing's hang-ups.

His name is Dr. Newlove, and he studied under Masters and Johnson before he decided to specialize in sex therapy for pandas.

Dr. Newlove agreed to talk but warned he would say nothing to violate a physician-patient relationship.

"I would say Hsing-Hsing is my most interesting case. If you look into his family history, he suffered from an overbearing Mandarin mother and a weak Cantonese father. He also was born right after the Cultural Revolution in China when making love was denounced as a capitalist bourgeois activity to distract the masses. This left a lot of scars on Hsing-Hsing."

"How do you plan to treat him?" I asked the good doctor.

"Slowly," he replied.

"Why don't you set up a television set in Hsing-Hsing's cage and show X-rated movies?"

"I know you're not going to believe this," Dr. Newlove said, "but pandas do not get turned on by human beings making love. The few times we've shown erotic films to pandas they started throwing orange peels at each other."

"It figures," I said.

"The ideal thing," he said, "would be to get some films of pandas making love to each other, but the only ones who have them are the Chinese, and they won't give them to us until we let them take back Taiwan."

"I know this is probably a chauvinist remark," I said, "but is it possible that Ling-Ling is to blame for Hsing-Hsing's impotence? Maybe she doesn't know how to excite him."

"There is always that possibility. Sometimes the female panda forgets her sensuality and does not look exciting when the male panda comes into the cage. I plan to have several sessions with Ling-Ling alone, teaching her to be more adventurous and more feeling. So far her idea of love play is to hit Hsing-Hsing over the head with her food bowl. Not all male pandas consider this a prelude to a seduction."

"Have you thought about water beds?" I asked him.

"I'm having one made now," Dr. Newlove replied. "Also, I'm trying to find a perfume that Hsing-Hsing might go for. Apparently, whatever Ling-Ling is using now is not doing the trick."

"It's too bad you can't use a surrogate wife," I said. "I read that sometimes that helps."

"I would if I could find one. My biggest problem is Hsing-Hsing has no one to compare Ling-Ling with. If I could get some fat, dowdy female panda in the cage, Hsing-Hsing might realize Ling-Ling is rather attractive and he could do a lot worse. But since all he ever sees is Ling-Ling, he takes her for granted. Hsing-Hsing honestly believes Ling-Ling is the only fish in the sea."

"If you can't do it," I told the doctor, "no one can."

"That's nice of you to say," he said modestly. "I know if I could get Hsing-Hsing into the marriage bed just once, he'd turn into a tiger."

EDUCATIONAL TELEVISION

The three major networks have announced that they're eliminating sex and violence on television from seven until nine o'clock every evening starting in September and will devote these hours to "family programs."

This means we're going to get all our violence between nine o'clock and eleven on the assumption that people who stay up past nine o'clock are not affected by the mayhem that the networks put on our screens every evening.

I don't know about you, but I'm much more concerned about the teenagers who watch television than the little tykes who have been shunted off to bed.

Last week I was at a friend's house watching a show with his son. The villain was making a time bomb out of four sticks of dynamite and an alarm clock. The bomber was meticulous in assembling the pieces, and the young man said, "Hmm. So that's how it's done."

"What do you mean?" I asked him.

"I never knew how to make a time bomb before. It's a snap."

"Why would you want to make a bomb?"

"To blow up a safe. Last night I saw a program about a bank, and they showed how you could break into it through the roof. But they couldn't get the safe open. I'll bet you with this bomb they could have done it."

"Didn't the bank have a night watchman?"

"Yeah, but they demonstrated how you could knock him out with one karate blow to the throat. You see, you take the palm of your hand and you go chop like this."

"Never mind," I said.

"Of course, if you don't want to use karate, there's a weapon now with two sticks and a piece of wire, and you throw it around the guy's neck and squeeze, and it's 'Good-bye, Charley.' "

"Where did you see that?"

"On some police show. This guy was really crazy. He killed about six people before they got him. They probably wouldn't have ever found him except for this girl he raped."

"They showed a man raping a girl on television?"

"Sure," my friend's son said with no surprise. "When you rape a girl, you should always grab her from the back and put your hand over her mouth so she doesn't scream. But you have to be careful she doesn't bite you, because later on her teeth marks could be used to identify you."

"Those are some shows you watch."

"What can I do? That's all there is. Do you know you can open anyone's lock with a piece of stiff cellophane? I saw it last Sunday. Look, let me show you."

"I believe you."

"Hey," he said, "if you ever go broke, I know how to burn down your house and collect the insurance without anyone finding out about it. I saw it Wednesday. You have to use cleaning fluid because it doesn't smell and. . . ."

"I don't want to know how to burn down my house."

"Okay. Last week I found out how you tap a telephone without anyone knowing it. It's really simple. All you have to do is find the panel box in an apartment cellar and adjust a few wires. You want me to demonstrate?"

"No, I don't want you to show me. Don't you learn

anything from television except how to commit a crime?"

"I saw a girl shooting up heroin two nights ago, but it turned me off."

"That's nice."

"Look! There's a chase. If you ever need anyone to drive a getaway car, I could do it with my eyes closed. Of course, if I had a motorcycle, they'd never catch me."

"I don't know why they call this entertainment, and the stuff on public television educational," I said. "You learn more in one week watching this claptrap than you do all year on educational TV."

"Wait until you see the movie coming up. It was made especially for television, and it shows you how to hijack a Boeing 747. I wonder if those things are hard to fly."

THE POLYESTER PLAN

A group of men were having lunch at a well-known restaurant in Washington the other day. Although they were in various professions, they all had one thing in common. They were away from home a great deal, and their wives had said they were getting fed up with it.

Amazingly enough it turned out that their wives, who did not even know each other, used the identical phrases when complaining about their lot.

These included: "All I'm doing is running a hotel."

"The only time I see you is when you come home to get clean laundry."

"You weren't even here for your own daughter's birthday party."

"What the heck is so important in ———?" (Fill in the city where you're going.)

It was at this juncture that Polyester, who works for a computer firm, sprung his plan.

"Our wives' main complaint," he said, "is that they have no one to talk to, which translates no one to bitch to.

The reason why we're missed is that they want someone to listen to their stories and give them moral support."

We all agreed Polyester's description of our wives was accurate.

"Suppose," he said excitedly, "we had a computer that could match up complaining wives with other husbands who were on the road?"

We all looked goggle-eyed.

"Are you suggesting wife swapping?" Acrilan asked.

"In a sense," said Polyester, "but no hanky-panky in the bedroom. You swap wives just so that they have someone to talk to. Let me give you an illustration. I'm on my way to Boston, and I feed the computer at National Airport the arrival of my flight and how long I'll be there. I also tell the computer how many children I have, my position in the firm and salary.

"The object of the computer would be to match me as closely as possible to my own situation at home. The computer gives me an address and phone number. At this very moment there is a man in Boston coming to Washington, D.C., and he goes to his computer and asks for an address here. He gets mine. Right?

"Okay. I get to Boston, and I check into my hotel. Now remember, the success of this scheme is no hanky-panky.

"Let's say my surrogate wife is Mrs. Dacron. I call her and ask when dinner is being served. I show up at the house at six P.M., and before I even get to hang my coat in the closet, Mrs. Dacron fills me in on the day. She tells me how lousy the kids have been behaving, what went wrong with the garbage disposal unit, how much she paid for eggs, and how she can't manage a family on my salary. I get an earful.

"At this very moment the man from Boston is at my house listening to my wife doing two hours on what it's like to run a house when the man doesn't even know where the fuse box is.

"Mrs. Dacron is thrilled to have someone there to let

out her frustrations on, and my wife finally has someone besides the kids to talk to."

"But what happens after dinner?" someone asked.

Polyester replied, "I go into the living room and watch television while Mrs. Dacron does the dishes."

"Don't you help her with the dishes?"

"Hell no. It would ruin it for Dacron if I did something he didn't do. Then, after watching TV, I go to my hotel. Dacron, who presumably let my wife do the dishes while he read the evening paper, also goes back to his place."

The trouble with Polyester's plan, when we all discussed it later, is that not one of us could find a single thing wrong with it.

CANADA, MY CANADA

I went to Canada the other day and was shocked to see that the Canadians were selling Cuban cigars.

"How can you sell Cuban cigars," I asked a friend in Toronto, "when the United States, your closest ally and friend, has an embargo on them?"

"What's wrong with selling Cuban cigars?" he asked.

"What's wrong with selling Cuban cigars?" I said angrily. "Don't you know that Cuba is a Communist country?"

"So is the Soviet Union," he replied. "That doesn't seem to bother you from selling Pepsi-Cola to them."

"That's different," I said. "We're selling Pepsi to the Russians because of the détente. We don't have a détente with Cuba."

"But the Soviets have been shafting you on practically everything since the détente. Yet you're giving them wheat and pushing their vodka in the United States."

"You're trying to confuse the issues," I said. "The Soviet Union is a major power. If we didn't give them wheat and Pepsi-Cola and didn't agree to sell their vodka, we might face a confrontation which nobody wants. Cuba is too small to give us any trouble; that's why we put an embargo on her cigars."

"Just out of curiosity, what good is the embargo on Cuban cigars?"

"It's our way of showing Cuba we will not stand for military dictatorships in the Western Hemisphere."

"What about the military dictatorships in Brazil, Chile, and Paraguay?" he asked.

"They don't make Cuban cigars," I retorted. "It seems to me that Canada should be as concerned about Communism as the United States."

"Well," said my friend, "if you're so concerned about Communism, how come you keep sending Kissinger to China?"

"One-third of the people in the world live in China. We can't ignore them even though we don't agree with their system of government. Besides, China is a long way from the United States. Cuba is just around the corner."

My Canadian friend was not convinced.

He said, "Do you know who buys most of the Cuban cigars in Canada?"

"Who?"

"Americans. The Americans come up here and smuggle them back into the United States."

"I don't believe you," I said. "No American would smoke a Cuban cigar while the embargo was on."

"It's true. Cuban cigars are much too expensive for Canadian tastes. Besides, we don't buy them here because they're too easy to get. But it's a big deal for an American to get a real Havana."

"If what you tell me is true, it's outrageous. I think Canada owes it to the United States to refuse to sell Cuban cigars to Americans."

"If you want to have a beef with Cuba," my friend said, "that's your business. But don't tell us who we can sell our cigars to."

"Someday when Castro is fighting on the beaches of Newfoundland, you'll remember what you said."

"By the way, do you want to smuggle back some Cuban cigars with you?"

"How much are they?" I asked.

"The cheapest Monte Cristos are a dollar apiece."

"All right, I'll take back one box with me just to show the people in Washington how fickle our friends in Canada really are."

IT ISN'T OUR FAULT

Just when I get my latent male chauvinist pig feelings under control, the new fashions come out and I'm back to where I started. Last week's cover of *Time* magazine of a girl in a black bathing suit made me forget the intensive consciousness-raising sessions I had attended all winter.

The trend for this year, if I understand it, is toward the pajama look with see-through fabric placed in areas you're not supposed to see. The backs are bare, and in many cases the midriffs are exposed. There is even a rain suit that zips down to the navel.

One has to assume that these clothes wouldn't have been designed unless the manufacturers thought women would buy them. And if this is the case, where do we men who have been trying to stop thinking of women as sex objects stand?

It is a terrible dilemma and one I don't think the women's lib people are facing up to. For example, the other night I went to a dinner party in Washington prepared to behave as the perfect liberated male. I was going to treat my dinner partners as human beings who had minds of their own and opinions on the subjects of the day that should be listened to.

Unfortunately, the person on my right was wearing a black net pajama top with a neckline that plunged down to heaven knows where. The blouse was held up by two tiny straps that looked as if they would break at any moment.

The person on my left was wearing what appeared to be a sheer scarf wrapped in such a way that her bosom was pushed up and out halfway across her soup plate.

Now you have to admit it's pretty difficult to discuss President Ford's tax-cut plans when you're faced with this kind of situation.

My heart said "These women have brains. Find out what they're thinking." But my eyes kept wandering down to areas other than their heads.

I wanted to talk about Jimmy Carter's chances in California and Scoop Jackson's hopes for New York with the person on my right, but all I kept thinking was: *I wonder what would happen if one of those tiny straps broke while she was reaching for a piece of roast lamb from the tray.*

I then turned to the person on my left to get such evil thoughts out of my head. I was going to ask her if she thought we should send wheat to Russia, but I noticed that the scarf she was wearing had shifted and there was even more cleavage showing than when she had sat down.

I was so ashamed of myself because I forgot all about Russian wheat, which I'm sure she would have been delighted to talk to me about.

I turned back to the person with the two itty-bitty straps. She had her back to me, which was bare all the way down to her lower spine. It just didn't seem to be the right time to talk about food stamps.

How, I pondered, *can I show these people that I am interested in their minds when I have so little to work with?* I would have given anything to have Gloria Steinem at my table to tell me what to do.

As I looked around the room, I noticed that all the men seemed to be having the same trouble. We were trying to make up for years of injustice and ignorance in our male attitudes toward the opposite sex, and they were doing everything to thwart us.

God knows we've all been sinners and most men are trying to change their attitudes toward women. But when you have nothing but bare backs and cleavage to stare at during dinner, how on earth can any man keep his mind on Henry Kissinger?

8

You've Flown a Long Way, Baby

THE LATEST FASHIONS

There is good news in the fashion world. If you really want to be a well-dressed woman this year, you can either go to Dior, Halston, Givenchy, Cardin, Bill Blass, or Goodwill Industries.

If you don't find what you want at Saks Fifth Avenue, I recommend the Salvation Army. What was going through the minds of the fashion designers this year is anybody's guess, but ugly is now beautiful.

I'm not certain how all these great minds arrived at the same tawdry clothes, but if they don't sell this year, you can't blame it on the recession. In the best of times no woman in her right mind would spend $350 for a dress when there is one exactly like it in her grandmother's trunk.

I am speaking from personal experience. The other day my wife came home with a box. In it was a dress I had seen in *War and Peace* (the war part), a hat from *Bonnie and Clyde,* and boots that were worn in *Doctor Zhivago*.

After she put them on, she said, "What do you think?"

"Don't tell me. You got a job as a scrubwoman at the Pentagon."

"This," she said haughtily, "is the droop look. It is à la mode for the winter."

"You could have fooled me. Are you sure the Russians aren't paying us back in clothes for all the wheat they bought from us?"

"I don't expect you to understand the fashion. The designers are sending us a message."

"The same one we sent Custer?"

"There is no sense in being surly about it. If you don't like the outfit, just tell me."

"It's fine, except that they forgot to sew the hem. It's down to your calves."

"That's where the hem is supposed to be."

"Well, your boots are falling down."

"They're not falling down. They're rumpled. They're squashed boots. They're supposed to look that way. You see, the shoe designers, when they heard the length of the skirt was going down so far, had to come up with a boot that would meet it. A regular boot would have gone to my knee. This one looks like it's falling, but it isn't."

"Bully for the boot people. Would you like to tell me what that long scarf is doing wrapped around your neck?"

"It goes with the dress. If I didn't have the scarf, you could see my blouse."

"What's wrong with your blouse?"

"Nothing's wrong with my blouse. But Paris and Seventh Avenue want us to wear long scarves this winter because it's going to be very cold."

"How did they know that last spring when they designed the clothes?"

"What about the hat?"

"I like the hat, but I can't see your face."

"You're not supposed to see my face."

"That's good. Hey, you know I've been trying to think who you look like."

"And whom do I look like?"

"Bess Truman—Harry's wife."

"Then I take it you want me to return the outfit?"

"Heavens, no. You never can tell when we're going to be invited to an Albanian wedding."

"Well, so much for the latest fashion."

"Don't get sore. I was only kidding. What coat do you wear with it?"

She put on the coat and stood there. I was amazed.

"My God," I said. "Columbo's gone into the fashion business!"

NO FRILLS ON THE AIRLINES

The "no frills" airline fare has gone into effect. National Airlines received permission to sell tickets on their planes for 35 percent less. Other airlines are expected to follow.

All the passenger would get on the plane would be a seat. He would have to bring his own food, his own drink, and provide his own Wash 'N Dry towelettes.

It's quite possible that the "no frills" part of the aircraft could be not only the most economical but the most fun as well.

I can see the scene.

Fifty people are seated in the back of the plane without so much as a stewardess in sight.

Each of them has a picnic basket or a box lunch on his lap.

As soon as the plane gets in the air, one of the passengers yells, "Does anybody want to trade a chicken salad with lettuce for a corned beef sandwich on rye?"

A man in the back says, "I'll give you a bacon, lettuce, and tomato for the chicken salad and throw in a hard-boiled egg."

His wife says, "I worked all morning to make the bacon, lettuce, and tomato sandwiches. How could you trade them for chicken salad?"

"I'll give you my corned beef sandwich," a man yells,

"for the chicken salad plus three brownies, and I can keep my pickle."

"Done," says the man with the chicken salad.

A couple set up a hibachi stove in the aisle and started to barbecue spareribs.

"Hey," says a man sitting across from them. "Are you sure you're allowed to barbecue ribs on the plane?"

The lady who was putting the barbecue sauce on the ribs says, "There's nothing in the ticket that says you can't cook your own meals in the no frills section of the plane."

"Well, in that case," replies the man, taking a sword out of his briefcase, "I'm going to have some shashlik."

The odors of the cooking start to permeate the cabin. A lady preparing a cheese fondue on the seat next to her asks the lady in front if she can borrow a cup of oil.

The lady gives her the oil in exchange for some sugar which she needs for her pancake batter.

By this time the passengers in tourist and first class smell all the food. An angry first-class passenger who has wandered into the no frills cabin by mistake comes storming back and says to the stewardess, "How come they're eating shashlik back there and we're eating this glop which you call chicken?"

"It's quite simple. If you have a no frills ticket, you don't get the airline's food."

"If we have to eat your food, we're the ones who should get thirty-five percent off," the first-class passenger says.

By this time all the passengers in the no frills cabin have finished their meals.

"What do we do for entertainment?" someone asks.

"I've got some great home movies of a trip we took to Greece," a man says.

"Great, let's see them," a lady says. "Then my son will play the guitar for you."

"We could have some singing afterwards."

"I have a bingo game if anybody wants to play."

A barrel of beer that one of the passengers had brought on board is opened, and paper hats are passed out by a party-favor salesman.

Several of the first-class and tourist passengers try to get back in the no frills section, but they are stopped at the curtain by the stewardess, who tells them sternly, "Go back to your seats, or I won't give you any coffee, tea, or milk."

GOD BLESS LITTLE OLD LADIES

What happened to all the little old ladies in tennis shoes? I am happy to report that they are alive and well, and most of them are on package tours in Europe.

Because traveling abroad has become so expensive, you do not see many Americans on the Continent anymore.

Occasionally a bearded kid with an American flag on the seat of his pants may walk by your café table, but it isn't like the old days when there wasn't a corner of Europe that didn't have a "U.S. Go Home" sign.

If it weren't for the little old ladies in tennis shoes, no one would be aware that the United States still existed, and it makes any red-blooded American's chest swell with pride when he sees a battalion of them marching down the Champs-Élysées, Piccadilly, or the Via Veneto to the tune of "Colonel Bogie's March."

Make no mistake about it, the little old ladies in tennis shoes still strike terror in the hearts of every tour director in Europe.

Most of the ladies are veterans of previous overseas tours—experienced in hand-to-hand combat at flea markets, versed in the skills of fierce haggling in souvenir shops, trained to assault churches and museums, and prepared for sneak attacks on any American Express branch in the country.

The cemeteries of Great Britain, France, Italy, the Benelux and Scandinavian countries are dotted with graves of tour guides who expired trying to keep up the pace set by these indomitable souls.

At airports all over Europe you see fresh young guides barely out of college, wearing their tour uniforms waiting nervously for their group to jump off the plane and encircle the city. Screaming, "We take no prisoners," the little old ladies, carrying their duty-free shopping bags from the previous airport, climb aboard their buses, determined not to miss one single thing included in the price of the tour.

No mountain is too high for them to climb; no fjord is too wide for them to cross. Heaven help the guide who forgets to stop for tea in Zermatt (included in the package) or leaves out a church in Montmartre. Let a waiter skip a salad course in Salzburg or a cheese plate in Brussels, and he'll get a karate chop he'll remember for the rest of his life.

In the last thirty years Europeans have seen their countries invaded by American, Japanese, and now Arab tourists. But none of them has ever shown the strength, the moral fiber, or the staying power of the little old ladies in tennis shoes.

Why do they do it? Why, when most Europeans have lost interest in tourists, when waiters and concierges and shopkeepers have become more surly, when most things are cheaper in the States, do the ladies keep traveling abroad?

The answer came from a little old lady sitting next to me at Fouquet's. "Someone has to carry on," she said simply.

"The young people can't do it because they don't have the money; the middle-aged people can't do it because they don't have the stamina. If it weren't for us little old ladies in tennis shoes, no one would remember what an American looked like. We've all taken a vow that as long as we can climb the steps of the Piazza di Espagna in Rome or wade on the beaches of Monte Carlo, we will see that the sun never sets on an American tourist. Besides, I promised my grandson a sword from Toledo."

I almost broke into tears. Twenty years ago the American traveler ruled Europe from Gibraltar to Helsinki. Our traveler's checks were coveted from Dublin to Istanbul. There wasn't an arcade in Venice or a bazaar in Athens that didn't have a sign ENGLISH SPOKEN HERE. Those were the golden days for Americans, and we may never see them again.

So let's hear it for the little old ladies in tennis shoes. God bless them for showing the flag in the Old World. As long as they have the money and the time and the grandchildren, the spirit of American tourism will never die.

A GREAT DISCOUNT OFFER

The airlines are going back into the discount business. Many of them are advertising special rates if you travel on Tuesdays, Wednesdays, and Thursdays, buy your ticket a week in advance, and stay where you're going for not less than seven days or more than thirty.

There is something wrong about this whole thing. Why should the airlines tell you how long you have to stay in one place in order to get a discount? It doesn't cost them any more to fly you there if you remain twenty-four hours or one year. If we let them get away with this, there is no telling what they'll demand of airline passengers next.

"I want to go to Los Angeles."

"Could you tell us the nature of your trip?"

"What business is that of yours?"

"If we consider it a good reason, we can give you twenty-five percent off on your ticket."

"What's a good reason?"

"That's for us to decide. We have a right to know what

you plan to do in Los Angeles if we're going to make it cheaper for you to fly there."

"I'm going cross-country skiing on Wilshire Boulevard."

"No jokes, please. Airline discounting is a very serious business. We can't give reduced rates to just *anybody*."

"Why not?"

"Because the idea of a discount is not to give old customers a break, but to attract new customers. For example, if you're a businessman and travel all the time on our line, there is no reason why we should make a lower price for you. You'll use us anyway. We're after the tourist who has never flown with us."

"You would think that businessmen would get the discount since they're your best customers."

"You're entitled to the discount if you stay seven days."

"Why seven days? Why not a month or a year?"

"Our computer discovered if you stay more than seven days and less than thirty, you probably had nothing serious on your mind. We wouldn't want you to just do what you had to do and then turn around and fly home. That wouldn't be very nice, would it?"

"I never thought about it before."

"Do you want the discount or don't you?"

"Yes, I imagine I do, though frankly I hadn't planned to spend seven days in Los Angeles."

"We won't tolerate perjury. If you say you'll spend seven days there and you don't, we'll find out about it. Our sales-promotion people are everywhere. Just last week a man said he would be in Miami for two weeks, and we gave him the full discount. Then one of our agents spotted him at Disney World in Orlando. We ripped up his ticket on the spot."

"Suppose I, in good faith, said I was going to remain in Los Angeles for seven days, but then something unexpected happened and I had to leave on Friday. Would that still be held against me?"

"You could appeal your case at the Airline Discount

Control Court in Burbank. But you would have to appear before the nine judges no later than seventy-two hours before you plan to leave Los Angeles."

"Suppose I don't tell anyone and just sneak on the plane?"

"There will be lie detectors at all the antihijacking search areas. You'll walk through a device, and if it shows your heart is beating too fast, federal marshals will take you to a room for questioning. We take a dim view of discount cheaters."

"What can you do to me besides make me pay the full fare?"

"Lose your luggage."

YOU'VE FLOWN A LONG WAY, BABY

Airline stewardesses have been complaining lately that they are not treated with enough respect by pilots and passengers. That may be so, but they're lucky they weren't working in the thirties. The Association of Flight Attendants has provided me with some of the rules that airline stewardesses had to obey in the early days of flying.

As you can see from the rules, the thirties were known by everyone except the stewardesses as the "golden age of flying."

"Remember at all times when on duty to maintain the respectful reserve of a well-trained servant. A ready smile is essential, but never permit yourself the intimate attitude of a 'traveling companion.' "

"Punch each ticket at each point passed." (Some flights involved up to thirteen stops.)

"Tag all passengers' baggage and check it on board."

"Remember to carry on board picnic baskets containing cold fried chicken, apples, rolls, cake, and vacuum flasks with hot coffee for passenger meals."

"Captains and pilots will be treated with strict formality

while in uniform, and a rigid military salute will be rendered the captain and the pilot as they go aboard and deplane. Check with the captain and pilot regarding their personal luggage, and place it aboard promptly."

"Wind the clocks and altimeters in the cabins."

"Keep the cabin windowsills dusted, and use a small broom on the floor before every flight."

"Check the floor bolts on the wicker cane seats in the Ford Tri-Motors to make sure they are securely fastened before each flight."

"A propeller in motion can be fatal to anyone who walks into it."

"Swat flies in the cabin after takeoff."

"Warn passengers against throwing lighted cigar butts out the windows particularly over populated areas."

"Face the rear of the plane when talking to passengers or serving lunch. Bending while facing toward the front of the plane tends to place the seat of your pants in the next passenger's face."

"Carry a railroad timetable just in case the plane is grounded somewhere."

"When slippers are available on long night flights, you will advise persons desiring to sleep as follows, 'I have slippers available, sir, if you would care to remove your shoes and rest your feet.'"

"Assist the passenger to remove his shoes, if he so desires, and clean the shoes thoroughly before returning them to him."

Now that, girls, I submit, was how to run an airline.

Everyone has his own favorite airline story from years gone by. My favorite took place in the late forties when I was flying from Belgrade to Zagreb in Yugoslavia. We were sitting on a DC-3 when one pilot got on board. There was no stewardess. The plane took off, and in a half hour the one pilot of the plane came back to the cabin and started serving coffee and candy sourballs.

We all gasped when we saw him walk out of the cockpit. The pilot grinned and said, "What's the matter? You people have never heard of automatic pilot?"

Paul Newman likes to tell the story of when he was with the Actor's Lab in Hollywood and they had an exercise. The problem the actors were told was that it was World War II, and the last plane to leave the Philippines was just about to take off. The fledgling actors and actresses were told to persuade the guards at the bottom of the steps that they had to get on the overloaded plane.

Each student made a passionate plea—one said she was pregnant; another that he had to report to the President; a third that he was needed by the Army. All their pleas failed. Finally one student actor ran up to the guards and screamed, "I have to get on the plane! I just have to get on the plane!"

"Why?" asked the guard.

"I'm the pilot!"

LOST LUGGAGE

One of the biggest problems of air travel is getting your luggage back at the end of the trip. For some reason more luggage is being lost now than ever before, and it's quite a headache for the airlines—not to mention the people who are flying.

What makes the whole thing mysterious is that if you're traveling with your wife, the airlines somehow manage to lose only *her* bags, the ones she absolutely needs if she is going to survive the trip.

There isn't a husband who has ever flown by air who hasn't faced this situation.

You get off the plane dog tired and wait at the baggage gate. The carousel keeps turning and turning with everyone's luggage. You have all your bags in a matter of minutes. Your wife gets all her bags except for one—the large garment bag with all her dresses, costume jewelry, and underthings. You wait an hour staring at the carousel, hoping against hope it will be the last piece of baggage off the plane. You don't dare speak to your wife. She finally speaks to you. "They lost my bag."

"I guess they did."

"What are you going to do about it?" she says, her lips pursed as if she's going to let out a scream.

"I am going to do *something* about it," you say, knowing in your heart there isn't a damn thing you can do. But you have to show some machismo. You go up to a man in uniform. "See here, sir," you say in your sternest voice. "You people have lost my wife's bag."

The man looks surprised. "I'm sorry, I'm the pilot of the plane."

There is another official-looking man with a badge on his chest. "Sir," you say, "you people have committed one of the gravest crimes known to tourism. You have lost the luggage of an honest woman. Unless you produce my wife's bag in the next thirty minutes, I shall have to report you to the president of your company."

"I'm a customs inspector," the man replies. "Go talk to someone from the airline."

Your wife, who is over in the corner twisting her handkerchief, asks, "What did they say?"

"I'm narrowing it down," you say. "The pilot of the plane doesn't know where your bag is, and neither does the customs service. So it must be someone else."

You are directed to a counter where one lone clerk is trying to cope with a large crowd of angry husbands. It is obviously the lost-luggage counter because all the women are huddled nearby wailing and tearing their clothes.

The clerk, hired for his masochistic tendencies, is smiling as he fills out long sheets of paper taking descriptions of the lost bags.

You get to the counter and ask the stupidest question any air traveler can pose: "Where is my wife's bag?"

The masochist smiles. "New Delhi, Bali, Rio de Janeiro. It could be anywhere."

"I have a good mind to slug you," you say.

"Oh, would you please?" he says. "Most people just shout at me, but very few of them really hit me."

"I wouldn't give you the satisfaction. What are we supposed to do now?"

"Why don't you go to your hotel and get a good night's sleep? If we find your luggage, we'll have it delivered."

"Suppose it's never found?"

"Then you can come back here and I'll fill out another form."

You return to your wife. "Well," you say, "it's no problem. They know exactly where the bag is, and you'll have it in the morning."

This calms her down until we get to the hotel. Then you make a mistake. As she's crawling into bed, you ask, "Where's your nightie?"

And she lets out a scream that can be heard all over the roofs of Paris.

ARRIVEDERCI, ROMA

"Don't go to Rome," I was warned. "Everyone is on strike." It was, of course, an exaggeration. When I got to the Leonardo da Vinci Airport, they were only having a slowdown, and it took me two hours to get my luggage.

"You're very lucky to get in," the taxi driver told me. "The airport employees are always going out on strike. They're very unhappy. The other day they went out on strike to protest the bad service everyone at the airport was getting. All the passengers had to find and carry their own baggage."

When I arrived at my hotel, I was handed a slip of paper.

"The employees will go out on strike from ten o'clock until four and from seven o'clock in the evening until eleven. We hope you will understand."

A friend picked me up in a taxi. "I would pick you up in my car, but it was stolen. Rome has the highest number of auto thefts of any city in the world," he said proudly. "Forty-two thousand were stolen last year, and only seven thousand were recovered."

"Where are we going?" I asked him.

"To the Vatican," he said.

"Are you taking me sightseeing?"

"No, I have to mail a letter. The Italian post office has had so many strikes that the only safe way to get a letter out of the country is by way of the Vatican post office. They set a special mobile lounge in St. Peter's Square just for mail. It's been so successful they should be able to pay all the costs for Holy Year."

"Rome sounds like a lot of fun."

"It is," he said. "The beauty of the city is that things have gotten so bad we don't know when people are on strike or not, because you don't notice any difference in the services."

"Why are the Italians always on strike?" I asked him.

"Oh, everyone has a different reason. The post office employees went out because nine of their fellow workers on night duty were suspended for bringing their cots with them and sleeping through their shift.

"I was at the Turin Airport last week and tried to check in with a couple of hundred people, including families, nuns, children, and businessmen. The clerk looked out at us and said, 'There are too many of you, and there is too much confusion. *Basta!*' And he and the six other clerks walked off, leaving us stranded for four hours."

We posted our letter and then went to a café. "The

Italian IRS has been on strike for five months. But it was their own fault. They made a big mistake when they let the IRS clerks read the returns of the chauffeurs who worked in their own ministry. The clerks discovered they were making two hundred thousand lire while the chauffeurs made eight hundred thousand. This got the clerks so mad they went out on strike."

"How can they keep going?" I asked.

My friend said, "The Romans are the greatest survivors of all time, and they're very well set up for strikes. The telephone company even has a number you can call, and they'll tell you who is on strike so you can plan your day around it."

"That's a good idea," I said.

"It is, except every once in a while the people who run the service go out on strike."

The waiter finally brought our coffee, after a half hour.

"Is he on strike?" I asked my friend.

"There's no way to tell," he replied.

My friend told me his favorite strike story. It had to do with the crew of an Italian Lines ship that had struck to get the same food as the passengers. The line gave in to the demands. At lunch they served the crew melon which they planned to give the passengers that night. The crew members said, "But the melon isn't cut. The chef must cut the melon."

The chef was called out of the kitchen, and he said, "I spit on your melons. I only cut the passengers' melons."

In protest the crew took their melons up on deck and dumped them into the sea.

"Things are getting so bad here," my friend said, "that all the American companies are pulling out."

"What about the Italian companies?"

"Oh, they left long ago."

9

Guess Who Came to Dinner!

A FAMILY SUMMIT

We all gathered in the living room for what was the first Family Economic Summit in our history.

I opened the meeting with a brief statement.

"I have called you all together to discuss the grave economic situation that this family faces. As you know, inflation has spiraled the cost of all consumer goods, and we could be heading for a serious domestic depression. I would like your advice as to how we can set our house in order."

My son, Joel, said, "I think your tight-money policies of the past year have contributed greatly to the crisis. It seems to me that if you loosened up on our allowances, it would give us more money to spend and take us out of our doldrums."

"I am not certain that is the solution," I replied. "One of the causes of the family economic woes is that we are spending more money than we're taking in. It was my hope that we could balance the budget before the year is out. Any increases in allowances at this time would only encourage inflation."

My daughter Jennifer said, "The biggest item in the family seems to be education. Why don't we all quit school and take a year off to find ourselves?"

"This is not a practical solution. If you took a year off

from school, I would have to subsidize you, which would cost more than your tuition. I hardly see a saving there. I don't believe a high unemployment rate in the family would solve anything."

I continued. "It seems to me one of the major causes of the problem is the high cost of gasoline. If everyone turned in his and her gas credit card and paid cash for your fuel, I could see a light at the end of the tunnel."

My daughter Connie said angrily, "A good transportation system in this family is essential to a healthy economy. Making us turn in our credit cards is an extreme measure, which should be used only when everything else fails."

"All right then, let us take up the subject of rock concerts. Last year members of this group spent a total of two hundred and fifty dollars on rock concerts and three hundred and thirty dollars on rock records and tapes. This is certainly an area where costs can be cut substantially."

Jennifer rose in a fury. "You are penalizing the poor and the neediest in this family by taking away from them their major form of entertainment. Why don't you cut some of the fat from Mom's household budget?"

"I was coming to that," I said. "It seems to me that too much money has been spent on slipcovers, drapes, and nonessential items such as lamps and rugs. I would suggest a five-hundred-dollar ceiling on all household expenditures."

"That's out of the question," my wife said. "Applying a meat ax to those few fixed cost-of-living items would only postpone what it would cost us to fix up the house at a later date. We are actually saving money by spending it now."

"I was afraid that would be your response. Well, what about food? Surely it would be no problem to cut there?"

"I would go along with that," my wife said, "with one stipulation. From now on you will do all the supermarket shopping for the family, which I'm sure you'd enjoy."

"Okay, let's forget about saving money on food," I

said. "But surely in this family budget there is some place we can cut waste."

My daughter Jennifer said, "Why don't you give up your season ticket to the Redskins' games?"

"Now, wait a minute," I replied angrily. "Let's not throw out the baby with the bath water."

GUESS WHO CAME TO DINNER!

I was invited to a state dinner by the White House in honor of Prime Minister Bhutto of Pakistan. This was the first time I ever went to the White House officially. The Fords keep inviting strange people to their parties, and the only thing White House dinner watchers can figure out is that they're working from an old Nixon enemies folder, which they mistakenly believe was the previous President's social list.

There is always the danger when a newspaperman is asked to break bread with a President and his lovely wife that he can be compromised. How can he partake of the food and wine and still keep his objectivity? This is a problem most White House press people have to deal with. I am happy to say that the Bhutto dinner has not affected my attitude toward the administration one bit.

I still believe President Ford is the greatest leader this nation has ever known. His economic program is flawless, and his budget is probably the clearest document since the Declaration of Independence.

It is inconceivable that a free-spending Congress would set up roadblocks in the way of the administration's program. In dealing with the recession and inflation, the President has presented the most comprehensive plan ever worked out by brilliant economists, oil experts, and financial advisers. If this program were adopted, prices would go down, employment would go up, and America would once again enjoy the prosperity and good life that it so richly deserves.

The problem, as I see it, is that Congress refuses to bite the bullet. Instead of joining forces with our great President, they are voting inflationary programs that could break the back of Mr. Ford's efforts to hold down government spending.

By voting day after day to reject the needed legislation to turn this country around, the Democrats are playing politics with the economy of the country.

It is inconceivable to me that our lawmakers would make a partisan issue out of the magnificent effort by the President to solve our temporary woes.

I have always had an open mind on the energy problems the United States faces. But after President Ford explained it to me, while we were drinking coffee, I am now convinced that the only answer to this nation's self-sufficiency is a $3 tariff on imported oil, deregulation of prices for domestic gas reserves, and a postponement of environmental regulations in favor of getting coal and oil out of the ground.

I had the good fortune of talking to Secretary of State Henry Kissinger at the same dinner, and it's lucky I did, because I have now concluded it was a mistake to cut off aid to Turkey, refuse arms to South Vietnam and Cambodia, and investigate the CIA.

Our foreign policy has been severely wounded by the ambitions of certain Democratic senators who have their eye on the White House in 1976. Congress must leave the President and Kissinger alone if we are to achieve the goals of peace that all of us so desperately pray for.

It was no accident that Secretary of Agriculture Earl Butz and I agreed over cognac and a cigar that his farm policies were the only ones that this country should follow. I couldn't believe that this fine man had been vilified by a scandal-mongering media that wouldn't know the truth if it was right in front of their eyes.

As I danced with Mrs. Ford after dinner, I decided I was glad I had accepted her invitation to eat at the White House. All my fears about being taken in by the administration were groundless. One meal cannot change a man's opinion of our President or his gracious First Lady. Not since Dolley Madison. . . .

SLEEPING BAG GENERATION

I was very surprised to read in the newspaper last week that Mrs. Ford said her family was cutting down on their food bills as a way of fighting inflation. The reason why I was surprised was that Mrs. Ford has teenagers, and there is no way under the sun that you can cut a food budget when you have teenagers living in the house. It isn't the immediate family that costs money—it's feeding everyone else's children that sends your food costs skyrocketing.

In the past most of us could get away with giving a strange child a glass of milk and a cookie. But in recent years we seem to be sustaining large masses of youth, which I have dubbed, for the want of a better name, the Sleeping Bag Generation.

Last month my grocery bill for a family of four on Martha's Vineyard was $791. This is what happened.

Three sleeping bags showed up at the door. A voice from one of the sleeping bags said, "We're very good friends of your daughter Hilda, and she said we could camp on your property when we got here."

"I have no daughter named Hilda," I said.

"What's her name?" a voice from another sleeping bag asked.

"Jenny."

"That's it," the voice said. "We're good friends of Jenny, and she said we could sleep on your lawn so we won't be arrested and tortured by the police with chains and rubber hoses."

"We won't be any bother," a voice from another sleeping bag said. "We have stale doughnuts for dinner."

I gave permission for them to camp out on the lawn. When my daughter came home, I informed her that three of her dearest friends had arrived and set up camp.

"Boys or girls?" Jenny asked.

"How the hell would I know?" I replied.

It turns out that sleeping bags require large amounts of nourishment. While those of us who lived in the house could get by on bluefish or eggs, the sleeping bags had to be fed steak, ham, imported cheeses, French bread, butter, and a good brand of beer.

Every day my daughter, who never did find out their names, carried down provisions to the sleeping bags. The zippers would open up automatically, and they would consume $60 worth of groceries at a feeding.

In exchange for the food, the sleeping bags strummed music on a guitar in our living room while I was trying to watch the evening news.

After the sleeping bags departed, a new group of sleeping bags arrived and said they were friends of my son Edward. I probably would have been nicer except I have no son named Edward. The nearest thing to it was Joel. While it bothered me, it didn't seem to bother Joel. He took all the sleeping bags to Kronig's grocery store, where they charged everything to me for a picnic they were holding with some other sleeping bags on the beach.

Now that I'm back in Washington, the sleeping bags are starting to show up here. Many turn out to be friends of the sleeping bags who camped on my property in Martha's Vineyard. If I refuse hospitality for them, I am considered an ogre by my children, Hilda and Edward, or whatever their names are. But if I let them spread out on the grass, I'm going to get another $800 grocery bill.

I'm sure Mrs. Ford is telling the truth when she says

she's been able to cut back on her food bills. But I figure the only way she has been able to do it is by having the Secret Service boot all the goose-feather sleeping bag acquaintances of her children right off the White House lawn.

OH DAD, POOR DAD

Poor President Ford. With all he has to worry about he also has to contend with everyone in his family speaking his or her own mind.

Any father can sympathize with what Mr. Ford has to go through every night.

I can just imagine the conversation at dinnertime in the White House when only the immediate family is there.

President Ford says, "Whew, what a day. I vetoed ten congressional bills, made three Republican fund-raising speeches, and had to show the emperor of Japan every bush in the Rose Garden."

Jack Ford says, "Dad, I have to tell you something."

"What is it, son?"

"Last summer I went skinny-dipping with a bunch of kids at Aspen."

"Was this before or after you smoked pot?" the President asks.

"I don't remember. I think it was after."

"This is too much. How does it look for the President of the United States to have a son that goes skinny-dipping?"

"But, Dad, you always told us to be frank with you and tell you exactly what we had on our minds. That's what holds this family together."

"I know that, and I respect you for leveling with me. But I have a tough election coming up, and there are a lot of people out there who don't approve of mixed skinny-dipping."

Jack says, "Mom said it was okay with her."

"I'm aware of it," the President replies.

Mrs. Ford says defensively, "Well, I would rather we know Jack goes skinny-dipping than have him sneak around and do it behind our backs. At least he's not a hypocrite."

"I agree," the President says, "but if this gets out in *McCall's* magazine, it's going to raise quite a ruckus."

"It won't get out in *McCall's,*" Mrs. Ford says.

"How can you be so sure?"

"Because the only one who knows about it is the *Reader's Digest.*"

"You told *Reader's Digest* that your children go skinny-dipping?"

"I didn't tell them until they asked me. I'm certainly not going to lie to *Reader's Digest,*" Mrs. Ford says.

"Why does the public have to know everything we do in this family?" the President asks.

"Because that's the way you brought us up," Susan Ford says. "Do you want to know what I did last night?"

The President says, "Can't I read about it in the paper tomorrow morning?"

"I photographed a topless waitress. Mom said it was okay."

Mrs. Ford says, "It was an assignment for the Associated Press, and David Kennerly was with her."

"Good grief," the President cries. "Don't you people have any secrets you can keep from me? Do I have to know *everything* you do?"

"Well," says Jack, "if you want us to have private lives, we will, but I don't see how you can trust your family if we can't take you into our confidence."

"Jack's right," Mrs. Ford says. "Some fathers don't even know when their daughters are taking the Pill."

"Who's taking the Pill?" the President shouts.

"Nobody," Mrs. Ford says, "but if Susan were, it would be nice if we knew about it."

"I suppose you said that to the *Reader's Digest* too?"

"I did not," Mrs. Ford says. "I told it to *Good Housekeeping*."

THE NEWS ON THE BEACH

Many people are discovering this summer that it isn't *what* you read but *where* you read it that counts. This was dramatically illustrated several summers ago at East Hampton, Long Island. I was lying on the beach, and the only thing between me and the Atlantic Ocean was a young lady in her twenties trying to get a suntan. In order to do this, she lay on her stomach with the top half of her bathing suit undone. This, I assumed, was so that she would get an even tan. As long as she stayed in her position, there was nothing to see but her back. But you never know what can happen on a beach.

"I see," my wife said, reading the paper, "that the failure of the SALT talks means that both superpowers are going to go full steam ahead on offensive missiles."

"What a pity," I said. As I saw it, my best bet would be if some little kid ran by and accidentally showered sand on the girl, forcing her to turn her body to find out what was going on.

My wife turned a page. "The bank rates are up to twelve and a quarter percent, and now they're predicting they'll go to thirteen percent. Herb Stein, the President's economic adviser, says the only one to blame for inflation is the American people. Do you think we're really responsible?"

"If he says so," I replied. There was another hope. If some bather came out of the ocean wringing wet and dropped water on her back, the shock of it might make the girl sit up.

"The White House transcripts don't jell with the ones

released by the House Judiciary Committee," my wife read. "Mr. Nixon certainly looks like he knew a lot more about Watergate than he admitted. Why is it taking them so long to impeach him?"

"That's a good question," I answered. My only other hope would be a cloudburst. The icy raindrops would certainly make her panic.

"It says here," my wife continued, "that Mr. Nixon's strategy, if the Supreme Court makes him turn over the tapes, will be to stonewall Jaworski, by saying it will take a lot of time to find the tapes and edit them. In that way the House Judiciary Committee won't have time to hear all the evidence before they're forced to vote. All he's doing is stalling. Doesn't it make you furious?"

"Live and let live, I always say."

"You don't seem very excited about the news," my wife said.

"I am, I am. Why is Mr. Nixon stonewalling Herb Stein?"

"He isn't stonewalling Stein; he's stonewalling Jaworski."

"Hmmm," I said. The dear girl seemed to be asleep. My only hope now was that she'd have a bad dream and wake up startled.

My wife continued reading the paper out loud. "The National Football League strike is still on. You might not be able to see the Redskins this fall."

"If you've seen one football game, you've seen them all," I muttered.

"Are you all right?" she asked.

"I'm fine. My neck hurts a little from the sun."

"You know," my wife said, "she's *not* going to move."

"Who?" I pretended to be surprised.

"That topless floozie over there." She folded up her newspaper neatly. "Anyway, even if she moved, it wouldn't have done you any good."

"Why not?"

"Because," she said sweetly, "I would have kicked sand in your eyes."

SUMMER INTRIGUE

I was glad to discover last weekend that Washington isn't the only place in the United States where people are all screwed up. Even a town as affluent and peaceful as East Hampton has terrible problems. We were houseguests of the Stones, and they asked us who of our dear friends in East Hampton we would like to see.

"How about the Grabowskis and the Peregrines?" I suggested.

"We can't have the Grabowskis with the Peregrines," Stone said. "It seems two years ago Grabowski borrowed Peregrine's barbecue spit and returned it the next day with the handle missing. Grabowski didn't mention it, much less offer to pay for a new handle, and so Peregrine hasn't spoken to him since."

"Well, what about the Cummerbunds?"

"*We're* not speaking to the Cummerbunds," Stone said curtly.

"I thought they were your best friends."

"They were until I played tennis with Tom Cummerbund last weekend, and he called a foot fault on me. You don't call foot faults on your friends. I've never called a foot fault on Tom in my life, and believe you me he foot faults all the time. He can't serve without having both feet in the court."

"Let's forget Cummerbund," I said. "I'd love to see the Wackenbushes."

"You can see him but not her," Stone said.

"Why can't I see her?"

"She ran away to Newport with a gardener."

"Was Wackenbush sore?" I asked.

"Not as much as Henry and Lucy Trilby. You see it

was *their* gardener. They're not talking to Wackenbush because they feel if he had paid more attention to his wife, the Trilbys' rhododendrons would still be alive."

"So much for the Wackenbushes," I said. "You know who we'd love to have dinner with—the Coffinbacks."

"You can have dinner with them," Stone said, "but we won't."

"But we all grew up with the Coffinbacks," I said.

"That's exactly the point. Two weeks ago we gave a dinner party for Ann Miller, the tap dancer, and we invited them. Then last weekend they gave a dinner party for Tony Martin, and you know what they did—they asked us to come in for coffee afterwards."

"Boy, this East Hampton is full of intrigue," I said. "I think it would be easier if you could tell me who we can see."

Stone thought for a while. "There's the Pattersons. We like them very much, and I know you do, too."

"Let's invite the Pattersons then," I said.

"They're not here," Stone said. "They rented their house for July and went to England. What about the Profiterolles?"

"I don't know the Profiterolles," I said, "but we'll see them anyway."

"Nah," said Stone. "They'd bore you to death."

"I don't see how you people make it through the summer," I said.

"It's not easy," Stone admitted. "There are a lot of people out here we'd love for you to meet, but we can't stand their houseguests. And there are a lot of houseguests we'd love to see, but we can't stand the people they're staying with."

"Why don't we just go to a Howard Johnson's for dinner and forget about it?"

"No way!" Stone said. "The last time I was there I had a fight with the manager, and I told him I'd never come back."

"I guess that just about does it," I said.

"Wait a minute. I just remembered, there's the Rucksacks," Stone said.

"You mean you know one couple in East Hampton that nobody is mad at?"

"They just moved out here last week, and no one has had a chance to get sore at them yet."

RESHUFFLING THE GUEST LIST

People take power very seriously in Washington, and when there is a major reshuffle in government, it really plays havoc with the social life of the town.

My wife and I were talking about it some months ago.

"Well, I guess we don't have to worry about inviting the James Schlesingers to dinner anymore," I said.

"That's a pity," my wife said. "He seemed like such a nice, intelligent man."

"Don't go sentimental on me now," I warned. "This is a cruel town. He just isn't one of Jerry Ford's guys."

"I guess you're right. I also hated to cut the William Colbys off our list."

"Well, we don't have to until December eighteenth. President Ford asked him to stay on at the CIA until then, so I can't see what harm it would be to have them over before Christmas," I told her.

"What are we going to do about the Henry Kissingers? I read in one of the columns that he had his wings clipped," she asked.

"Henry does present a problem," I admitted. "He's still secretary of state, so we can't cut him off completely. Besides, he has great survival powers. Probably the best thing to do, until the dust settles, is invite him for cocktails and buffet. But let's wait awhile before we consider him for a sit-down dinner."

"That's a pity," she said, "because Henry is a lot of fun at a sit-down dinner."

"He was a lot of fun when he was both secretary of state and the head of the National Security Council. But I don't know how much fun he'll be now that he has only one job. Why don't we leave it like this? We'll invite him for cocktails and buffet, and if people don't seem to object, then we can put him back on our sit-down dinner list."

"That's a good solution," my wife said happily. "We'll let Washington decide for us. Now what do we do about the Rumsfelds?"

"From all reports they're coming up fast. I think we should have a black-tie party for them," I said.

"Do you think they'll come? We never paid much attention to Rumsfeld when he was working in the White House," my wife said.

"It wasn't our fault. At the time we didn't know how important he was. I thought he was just another pretty face in the White House."

"Well, you should have been more aware of what he was up to," my wife said accusingly. "We look awfully silly calling them now after they've been in Washington for more than a year."

"It was a mistake, but we'll make it up to them. We'll invite Barbara Walters to the same dinner."

"That could do it," my wife said.

"Should we invite George Bush to dinner?"

"Of course. What a stupid question to ask."

"It's not that stupid," she said. "When he was posted to China, you said he was going nowhere and we could forget about him."

"How did I know he was one of Jerry Ford's guys? Send the invitation to Peking so we get in ahead of all the social climbers in this town."

"I think I ought to write to the Elliot Richardsons in

London, too," she said. "They'll probably be in demand as well."

"That's a good idea," I replied. "Particularly since he's one of the people they're talking about for Vice President."

"Which brings us to the Rockefellers. What do we do about them?"

"I was afraid you'd ask me that. I'll tell you how I feel about it. Rocky can't do us any good now, but a lot of people are going to cut him off. And even though we'll be open to criticism from certain conservative quarters, I think we should still let him come for lunch."

My wife kissed me on the forehead. "You're all heart."

10

We Have a File on You

THE FIRST WIRETAP

A great deal has been written about the man who invented the telephone, but very little has been said about the first man to tap one. As everyone in law enforcement knows, the telephone is absolutely worthless unless you can find out what the people on each end of the line are saying.

The man who gets full credit for having tapped the first telephone line anywhere in the world is J. Edgar Soosa, a young agent in the Justice Department during President Ulysses S. Grant's administration.

Soosa was not only a dedicated law enforcement officer but a whiz at electronics. He believed that when fighting crime, domestic and foreign, you had to use every weapon at your disposal. It was thanks to Soosa's determination and skill that anyone can now tap a telephone in this country without fear of detection or retribution.

This is what happened: In 1875 Ulysses S. Grant was finishing out his term of office. Grant was hoping to run again in 1876, but he was worried about his political enemies, who he believed were everywhere. One in particular was an Alexander Graham Bell, a Scotsman who worked in Boston. Someone at the White House had told President Grant that Bell was working for the election of Rutherford B. Hayes. (The aide actually had confused Alexander Graham Bell with a Boston politician named

Arnold Choate Bell, who was a big Hayes supporter.)

President Grant called in J. Edgar Soosa and told him, "This is very confidential, but I want you to go to Boston and find out what Alexander Graham Bell is up to.

"When you get the information, I want you to report directly to me. Use any method you have to as long as you get results. If you get caught, I'll see that you get an executive pardon."

Soosa, who was used to following orders, immediately proceeded to Boston. He discovered that Alexander Graham Bell was working with deaf children, which obviously was a cover for his real job, which was to get Rutherford Hayes elected President.

Bell lived in a boardinghouse with an assistant named Thomas A. Watson. Soosa rented a room in the same house under the name of Zimbalist.

When both Bell and Watson went out one day, Soosa broke into their rooms. He discovered a series of wires going from one room to another. They were connected with strange-looking speakers. His curiosity was aroused. Why were Bell and Watson communicating by these wires when their rooms were only 100 feet apart? It was obvious that they were afraid that if they were in the same room together, they might be overheard.

Soosa reported his findings back to President Grant, who became terribly perturbed. "We have to know what they're saying to each other," he said.

Soosa agreed. "I've been thinking about it. If I could attach a wire to their wire and have a speaker in my room, I could record everything they say."

"Then do it," Grant thundered.

"There's only one problem," Soosa said. "It may be illegal. I'm not sure you can attach a wire to somebody else's wire and listen in."

"Dammit," said the irritated President. "The national security of the United States is at stake. I want to know what they're plotting."

Soosa went back to Boston and attached a wire to Bell and Watson's. All during winter he sat with earphones on his head, but the line was dead. Then finally, on the morning of March 10, 1876, Soosa's patience was rewarded. Over the line he heard Bell shout, "Mr. Watson, come here. I want you."

Soosa immediately took the tape to Washington, D.C., and while Grant sat drinking a whiskey, the agent played back the immortal words.

Grant smiled. "Just as I suspected. They were out to get me. Mr. Soosa, you have made a great contribution to your country. In years to come every President will owe you a debt of gratitude and say, 'Thank God for Soosa, who made the first wiretap possible.' Without you, sir, the telephone wouldn't be worth a damn."

WHERE ARE MY FILES?—PART I

Everyone worth his salt in Washington believes the FBI, CIA, State Department, and IRS keep voluminous files on him. Most people may pretend they're furious about anyone monitoring their activities. But in their hearts it's a great ego builder to know that Big Brother considers them important enough to keep tabs on them.

I have to confess I also have felt this way. In my fantasies I have always thought that there is a giant computer buried at Mount Weather in the West Virginia mountains whose sole function is to keep track of everything I write, say, or do. This computer is working day and night and is being fed by thousands of federal bureaucrats who have been assigned to me because I am considered the most dangerous man in Washington.

Soon after the Freedom of Information Act was passed, making it possible for American citizens to demand to know what data the government kept on them, I wrote letters to the FBI, CIA, State Department, and IRS requesting my files. I offered to pay the cost of research (each agency has its own rate card) and told them I expected the information within ten working days, as the law provided.

All of them responded to the request and said they would get back to me as fast as possible.

As I read their letters I imagined the chaos I was causing at State, Langley (CIA headquarters), the FBI, and the IRS.

Meetings were probably going on to discuss how much information could be released without hurting national security.

I was sure Henry Kissinger would insist on dealing with my State Department files personally. Bill Colby at the CIA would have to call back Dick Helms from Teheran. Clarence Kelley would pull a dozen agents off the Patty Hearst search to comply with my request, and the IRS would have to stop giving rebates in order to make the ten-day deadline.

But ten days later I heard from the four agencies. They all needed more time. Robert Young, whose title at the Central Intelligence Agency is Freedom of Information Co-ordinator, wrote, "I assure you that we are continuing to process your request, but this work has not yet been completed. We have received hundreds of requests, each of which requires a thorough search of records and *a thoughtful review of any material located*" (my italics).

Barbara Ennis of the State Department wrote that my file was at the Federal Records Center in Suitland, Maryland, and retrieval would take longer than expected.

Clarence Kelley of the FBI wrote me personally (at least his signature was on the letter), telling me it would take at least thirty days to find my files (no wonder they were having so much trouble finding Patty Hearst).

I decided to give them all the extension they asked for out of the goodness of my heart. I assumed there was so much data on me no agency could find everything in the ten-day period.

But I must say I was starting to worry about my government. Suppose I were a spy or a tax evader or an agitator. It seemed to me I could skip the country before anyone could get their hands on my files. I made up my mind that after I got the information they had on me, I would call for a complete investigation of all federal filing systems.

The following days were pleasant ones for me. I kept thinking of all those people in government poring over my data, working late into the night, collating the raw files that they had collected over a period of twenty-six years.

There would probably be shocks and gasps from the younger researchers who weren't used to handling such sexy stuff. But I figured if they were in the Freedom of Information business, they would have to get used to it.

Just as I was about to lose hope, the first file arrived. It was from the CIA. My hands trembled as I opened the large brown envelope. I started to read. *(To Be Continued)*

WHERE ARE MY FILES?—PART II

Having applied to the CIA, FBI, IRS, and State Department for any files they had on me under the Freedom of Information Act, I waited anxiously for them to arrive. The first envelope, after a twenty-day wait, came from the CIA. I must say I was disappointed because I expected a much bulkier package. After all, I had been stationed abroad for fourteen years in Paris, and I assumed they had kept daily track of all my activities.

It turns out it was terribly meager pickings. The first item was a report from the Soviet Union quoting a Moscow radio station quoting me about something innocuous

I had written about the CIA in my column. I only received one mention in the three-page memorandum which was hardly worth the price of the Xeroxed pages.

The second piece of paper in the file was a memorandum from Cord Meyer, Jr., dated June 9, 1964. At that time Meyer's title was Chief of Covert Action Staff. I knew Meyer worked for the CIA, but I wasn't sure what he did. We used to meet at parties, and I was always sounding off about one thing or another just to make it look as if I knew something.

From the memo it appeared that Meyer had had a conversation with Senator Eugene McCarthy and myself.

Meyer's conversation with McCarthy had been omitted, but mine was reported. It said, "Mr. Buchwald added that it was his feeling that the policy control over the agency was not as close as it should be. He cited as an extreme example the claim of the Cuban exiles in the recent 'Bay of Pigs' that they had been encouraged to proceed with the invasion even if the White House issued contrary orders. I stated that I was not personally familiar with the Cuban events, but it was my clear understanding that no such incitement to mutiny had ever been officially authorized, and that it was inconceivable to think that it had been."

That was it! My entire CIA file. One lousy mention of the Soviet radio and a stupid conversation at a party with one of the agency's chief spooks when I was probably quoting *Time* or *Newsweek* magazine. Either the CIA had no interest in my activities, or they had held back everything from the folder and sent me a few cigar ashes.

I was heartbroken. If I had known Cord Meyer, Jr., was reporting back to headquarters on what he heard at parties, I sure as hell would have come up with something more interesting than some idle gossip about the Bay of Pigs.

To add insult to injury, the next day I received a letter from the Internal Revenue Service which said, "Please be advised that we checked the indices of the former Special Service Staff and the Baltimore District Intelligence Gathering and Retrieval System. These indices failed to disclose the existence of any record relating to Art Buchwald."

I couldn't believe it. Here I was, one of the foremost critics of the Johnson and Nixon administrations, and the IRS claimed it didn't have one piece of derogatory paper on me.

Before I could digest this, I heard from Barbara Ennis at the State Department. She informed me that if I sent a check for $21.50, she would send me everything the State Department had about me.

I immediately dispatched $21.50 and waited breathlessly for the file. It arrived a week later. I'm almost ashamed to tell you what was in it. There were six Xeroxed copies of my passport applications over the past twenty-six years and a letter from George Ball asking me if I would like to have lunch with him sometime. You'll have to admit that isn't much to show for someone who has knocked the heck out of American foreign policy for a quarter of a century.

So there you have it. In spite of the Freedom of Information Act, it's obvious no one in the government wants to tell me what they really have in their files on me. The big question is why. Is the stuff so hot that no one will take the responsibility for releasing it? Or perhaps the true files are in still another computer which the CIA, IRS, and State Department don't know about. I can't believe someone who has had as exciting and meaningful a life as I have would be so totally ignored by the intelligence-gathering agencies of the United States.

My only ace in the hole is that I still haven't heard from Clarence Kelley at the FBI. Knowing J. Edgar Hoover's penchant for details, I'm certain when the FBI sends over its files on me, it'll have to deliver them in a

U-Haul. I can hardly wait, because I want to see if the FBI's reports on my sex life are as terrific as mine.

THE FBI UNDERCOVERED

I couldn't believe the story in the newspaper when an FBI informer revealed that he had infiltrated the Ku Klux Klan with orders to sleep with the wives of Klansmen to get information and sow dissension in the Klan's Klaverns.

But it was confirmed to me by another informer who came to my office with a paper bag over his head.

"I'm glad it's all out in the open," he said as I helped him sit down in the chair. "I've done terrible things in my time, and now I no longer have to keep it to myself."

"Let's start at the beginning," I said. "You worked as a Klan informer for the FBI?"

"That's right. You could say I moonlighted for them."

"And what exactly were your duties?"

"My orders were to sleep with the wives of Klansmen and get information and also sow dissension."

"You're not the same person who testified on the Hill the other day?"

"No, that was Gary Rowe. He worked in Alabama. My territory was Georgia, from Savannah to Stone Mountain."

"That's a lot of territory to cover."

"You can say that again. I was really dragging at the end of a week. After about two months I asked to be transferred to the U.S. Communist Party instead."

"Why?"

"It was less physical, if you know what I mean. The Commies don't believe in marriage, so the FBI doesn't care about us making it with their wives."

"I hate to pry, but how did you meet the wives of the Klansmen?"

"Mostly at cross burnings. We'd all have our sheets on,

and I'd go up to one and say, 'Hey, don't I know you from somewhere?' "

"But if you had your sheets on, how would you know it was a woman?"

"From the shoes. The FBI taught us to always look at the shoes at a Klan meeting. If the person with the sheet is wearing high heels, seven out of ten chances it's a woman."

"So then what would you do?"

"You'd get to talk to her, you know. You'd ask her if she'd like to have a beer after the effigy hanging."

"What about her husband?"

"Well, that's just it. Ku Klux Klan members are usually out all night, riding around threatening blacks and burning down barns, and their wives get pretty lonely. So when a guy comes up to them wearing a sheet and invites them out for a beer, they're pretty flattered."

"And then what?"

"Well, you have a few beers, and one thing leads to another, and before you know it, she's telling you what a drag it is to be married to a member of the Ku Klux Klan because he's always out somewhere trying to scare the hell out of somebody."

"I guess being a Ku Klux Klanner's wife isn't what it's cracked up to be."

"You can say that again," my informant muttered through his paper bag. "If you knew how many of them hunger for just a little love and affection."

"How do you know how lonely they are?"

"You can see it in their eyes, which incidentally is the only thing you can see when they're in uniform."

"So, playing on this weakness, you were able to get information and create chaos in the Klan."

"They didn't pull the wool over my eyes," he said proudly.

"Let me ask you one more question. Did you ever get emotionally involved with any Klansman's wife?"

"Nah, when you see one Kluxer's wife, you've seen 'em all."

THE FBI'S BICENTENNIAL EXHIBIT

The FBI has finally firmed up its plans as to what it will do to help celebrate the country's Bicentennial.

Efrem Zumguard, the agent in charge of American Revolutionary Activities, told me, "The FBI plans to have one of the biggest exhibits of any government institution. We are going to put on display for the first time our top-secret files on George Washington, Thomas Jefferson, John Adams, Alexander Hamilton, and Francis Lightfoot Lee."

"I didn't know the FBI still had those files," I said.

"They were found in J. Edgar Hoover's office. He never threw anything away. We also have a very interesting slide show on Benjamin Franklin's sex life."

"Wow. I'd like to see that."

"There isn't anything about the American radicals we didn't know. We have photographs of everyone who participated in the Boston Tea Party, and one of our agents infiltrated Washington's rabble and got the names and addresses of everyone who crossed the Delaware."

"Then you must have known about Paul Revere?"

"Of course, we knew about Paul Revere. Our agents bugged his horse, and when he rode from Lexington to Concord, we got tapes of him shouting, 'The British are coming.' We also had the Old North Church under surveillance for months. When the signal flashed from the belfry, Hoover knew about it in forty-eight hours."

"You people were really on the ball."

"We're going to devote one whole wall to Thomas Paine. He was the worst agitator this country has ever known. Hoover was on to him from the start. We have the original copy of *Common Sense,* the most subversive document that was printed in the last two hundred years."

"More subversive than the Declaration of Independence?"

"Maybe it would be a toss-up. We're going to have a room set aside for the Declaration of Independence, which, incidentally, Hoover considered his greatest case. He knew everything that was going on in Philadelphia. The files on the Second Continental Congress would make your hair stand on end. Did you know Jefferson wore a wig and high-heel shoes when he wrote the Declaration?"

"No, I didn't."

"Hoover did. That's why Jefferson couldn't fire him. "You heard about Betsy Ross and Lewis Morris?"

"Not the Lewis Morris of New York?" I whistled.

"Hoover had pictures of them."

"Before or after she made the flag?"

"During."

"What about Lafayette?"

"He had an illegitimate child by John Paul Jones' wife. King George the Third really chuckled when he read that one."

"I guess there was no one in the government Hoover didn't know about."

"Do you know the first letter ever sent by the Continental Post Office? We opened it. It was from Jane Fonda's great-great-great-grandmother to Nathan Hale."

"I knew Hoover was diligent, but he seemed to have a sixth sense about things. No wonder everyone in the Thirteen Colonies was afraid of him."

"Now do you want to hear of the *pièce de résistance* of our exhibit?"

"Of course."

Zumguard said, "Remember the famous painting of 'The Spirit of '76'? Hoover had the original in his files. Do you recall the boy on the left playing the drums?"

"Yes."

"He was an FBI undercover agent. That's how we managed to convict the other two."

WE HAVE A FILE ON YOU

Several years ago I predicted that there were so many computers in operation in the United States that there would soon be a data famine in the country. I said that, unless new methods were developed to produce data, computer people would soon be fighting each other and possibly resorting to violence to get enough information to satisfy the appetites of their machines.

Unfortunately, I predicted this data war would start in 1984. Little did I realize it had already begun.

Everyone holds the FBI, the IRS, the CIA, local law enforcement agencies, as well as credit companies, responsible for invading the privacy of American citizens. But these organizations are not to blame. The responsibility rests with the computers which they have bought or leased that have to be fed constantly to justify their existence.

Let us take the FBI, for example. They purchased their computers to keep track of criminals and subversives in the United States. In no time the computers had absorbed the name and description of every racketeer, car thief, bomb thrower, and cattle rustler in the country.

Every scrap of information had been thrown in, but the computers kept demanding more. Frantic FBI officials sent out telex messages to their field offices: URGENT —SEND US EVERYTHING YOU HAVE IN YOUR FILES. COMPUTERS ARE DESPERATE FOR NEW DATA. NO MATTER HOW INCONSEQUENTIAL OR NONVERIFIABLE WE WILL TAKE IT. DIRECTOR INSISTS EACH FIELD OFFICE RESPONSIBLE FOR ONE TON OF RAW DATA PER WEEK. IF YOU FAIL TO MEET QUOTA YOU WILL BE SENT TO BILLINGS, MONT.

The FBI field offices tried to obey. All waste paper was

sent to Washington. Agents broke into local police station offices to steal their files; foreign embassies were rifled; union records were filched. But still, many of the G-men could not make their quota. So they started sending in information on citizens who had nothing to do with crime or subversion. Some field agents sent in entire telephone books from their areas; others made reports on members of the American Legion, the Elks, the Shriners, and the Daughters of the American Revolution. A few agents were so hard pressed they mailed in raw files on their own wives and children.

But the FBI computers kept chewing up the information at a faster rate than anyone in the bureau could produce it. There was talk of putting the computers on a six-hour day and operating them only four days a week. But when the computers heard about this (an agent had fed the suggestion into a computer to find out if it was feasible), red lights started to flash all over the computer center, and a readout indicated that if their work time was cut, every FBI machine would self-destruct in protest.

It was then decided the only way to assure a sufficient supply of data was to keep files on everybody, from college students to people on Social Security. Experts figured that if the FBI could get enough data on them, they could keep the computers busy until 1976. That is the only reason the FBI has your name on their list right now.

The CIA faced the same crisis as the FBI did, but it had a problem because by law the CIA is not supposed to keep files on American citizens.

After twenty-five years the CIA had tons of information on every country in the world, and although it occasionally was able to come up with fresh data, it was not enough to satisfy the voracious appetites of their machines, which incidentally were much larger than those of the FBI. Several years ago the CIA had no choice but to start feeding information on Americans. When Congress found out about this, the CIA had to suspend this operation, which left them in a pickle. Their computers were becoming restless and surly, and their printouts indicated there could be an in-house revolt.

So last month the CIA chiefs realized they had no choice. In order to get enough data for their computers for the next three years, they decided to do a psychological profile on every man, woman, and child in the People's Republic of Red China.

GOOD BUSINESS FOR CIA

Many stories have come out about the CIA, but this is one that is still buried secretly in the archives. It has to do with an agent named Greensleeves. He was young, energetic, and imaginative. The CIA decided to set him up in a souvenir shop across the street from the palace of a South American dictator, where he could keep tabs on the comings and goings of government officials.

They gave him enough money to buy the shop and the souvenirs so the operation would be legitimate. This exchange of cables, after they were decoded, tells the story.

"CIA Headquarters, Langley: Business excellent. Have sold $16,000 worth of souvenirs thanks to Dictator Tacos three-day anniversary celebration in front of palace. Please tell our people in Taiwan I need more Tacos ashtrays, paperweights, and letter openers. If all right with you, am planning a sale on Dictator Tacos music boxes that play 'South of the Border.'—Greensleeves."

"Greensleeves, Paella, South America: Glad to hear you are doing well businesswise, but what the hell is going on at the palace? We hear Tacos may be overthrown by right-wing colonels. Please advise at once.—Frogmaster."

"CIA Headquarters, Langley: Sorry I have been too busy taking inventory to pay much attention to palace, but have good news. Discovered a factory outside Siesta that makes cuckoo clocks and hand-painted scarves. Have bought three gross at half-price. Expect sales figures in June up 20 percent over May. Had to pay off customs to get cigarette lighters into country, but will add bribe to price of item.—Greensleeves."

"Greensleeves, Paella, South America: Why no word from you on Tacos assassination attempt and his exile from country? Who is now in charge of Paella? Urgently need list of junta and whether it's pro- or anti-American. —Frogmaster."

"CIA Headquarters, Langley: Agency has nothing to fear from Tacos overthrow. I got wind of it two weeks ago and had Tacos Birthday Sale on Saturday, where I marked down all Dictator Tacos items 50 percent. The bronze busts moved especially well, as did Tacos pillowcases. We also unloaded 4,000 plates with portraits of Mrs. Tacos. Only item that didn't sell as well as expected was night-light of Tacos standing next to Virgin Mary. But I plan to remove Tacos and just sell them as Virgin Mary night-lights. Tell our Hong Kong people that I am sending them photograph of Colonel Chili which I would like them to have framed with sea shells. Also need 3,000 beer mugs commemorating the junta's revolution of July 5. By the way, tell our Hong Kong man to check packing. The ashtrays they sent came in all damaged. Am seeing insurance company tomorrow—Greensleeves."

"Greensleeves, Paella, South America: What information do you have concerning naval attack on Paella by neighboring country of Enchilada? Understand shelling destroyed half of downtown as well as Soviet, British, French, and Chinese embassies.—Frogmaster."

"CIA Headquarters, Langley: Your information correct. I heard about it ten days ago from Enchilada defector and moved all breakable items to the basement. Also boarded up windows. You'll be happy to know we had the only souvenir shop in Paella that opened for business the next day. Since the invasion started, I have added a toy line with tanks, soldiers, missiles, and fighter planes. Believe they will be big sellers. Took it on myself to give 10 percent discount to any Paella soldier or sailor in uniform. Have also ordered music boxes which say 'Mother' on the top in Spanish. Understand Mother items sell well in time of war."

"Greensleeves, Paella, South America: What has happened to U.S. ambassador? Is he being held hostage by revolutionary urban guerrillas as reported by AP, UPI, Reuters, and Agence France Presse?"

"CIA Headquarters, Langley: U.S. ambassador was kidnapped three days ago. One of my salespeople has a brother who told her about kidnapping plans last week. I immediately took steps to check his charge account. He owed us $89. On a ruse that we were collecting accounts receivable early this year, I managed to get his check before he was grabbed. We haven't lost a dime on him. Any chance of shipping Fidel Castro coffee mugs? They're expecting 15,000 male Cuban tourists, and it could be a big item this summer."

THE RAW FILES OF THE FBI

FBI Director Clarence M. Kelley has said in a speech that collecting information about private citizens is not a serious threat unless the data are misused. And there, as Hamlet's masseur would say, is the rub. What guarantees are there that the raw files will not be misused? Suppose you have a vindictive computer which has in its memory bank the files on some of our leading citizens. Director Kelley may say it can't happen, but it did just last week. I was on a tour through FBI headquarters when I fell behind and this computer started chattering on its printout.

"Would you like to hear about a senator who wears

silk stockings and high heels when he's working on tax reform at home?"

I was shaken and punched back, "Of course not."

The computer's typewriter worked again. "There's a certain female movie star who takes baths in Coors beer with a well-known professional football player."

"What's so strange about that?" I typed back.

"Nothing, except he poses for Schlitz beer commercials," the printout read, "and always says, 'When you're out of Schlitz, you're out of beer!' "

"Oh, for heaven's sakes," I typed back, "don't you have anything better to do than just print gossip about people?"

The computer seemed to ignore my message and came back with, "There's a liberal actor in *The Towering Inferno* who sneaked off for a weekend to Lake Tahoe with a right-wing married actress from the same picture."

"Do you have proof of this?"

"No," the computer replied, "but where there's smoke there's fire."

And its lights started blinking as if it were enjoying its own joke.

I typed back, "I think this is disgraceful. You have all this material stored in you, and none of it has been verified. You could do tremendous damage to innocent people."

The computer's lights turned dark red. It was angry. "There are no innocent people. There are only Americans we know things about and Americans we don't," the printout read. "I am the keeper of the skeletons in everyone's closet."

"But just because you have it in your memory bank," I protested, "doesn't make it a fact."

"That's what you think. Once the raw files are fed into a computer it becomes the gospel truth. Computers never lie. Have you heard about the Supreme Court justice who took his wife to see *Deep Throat*?"

"What's so wrong with that?" I typed back.

"Six times?"

"Lies, all lies." I hit the keys furiously. "Your tapes are filled with rumor, innuendo, and vicious gossip. Don't you have any shame at all?"

The lights turned red again. "No one has ever called me a liar before."

"You're a disgrace to IBM," I angrily typed back. "Thomas Watson would be turning over in his grave if he knew the filth you had stored in you!"

The lights turned green. "Would you like to know what I have on you?" the printout read.

I turned white. "What could you possibly have on me?" I typed out with my fingers shaking.

The computer clicked noisily. "The Allegheny stewardess in Little Rock."

I almost broke my fingers. "I've never been in Little Rock in my life."

"Then maybe it was Kansas City."

"Allegheny doesn't fly to Kansas City," I typed back.

"Then maybe it was the Hertz Rent-A-Car girl," the computer replied. "I can't remember everything."

KILLING SANTA CLAUS

A group of CIA people were having coffee out at Langley Headquarters the other morning and discussing the Church report on their covert activities.

They naturally were outraged.

"They're destroying our intelligence capability," one executive said.

"They're wrecking morale," another chimed in.

A third man said, "It's like killing Santa Claus."

"Santa Claus!" their chief said in horror. "We forgot Santa Claus. What contingency plans do we have for eliminating Santa Claus?"

There was silence in the room. Then one of the men said, "Why Santa Claus?"

"It isn't our job to say, 'Why Santa Claus?' We have to have a plan ready in case someone in the White House or the State Department decides Santa has to be terminated with extreme prejudice. What have we got on him?"

"One of our agents at the North Pole says he's planning a sneak attack by reindeer on the night of December twenty-fourth."

"How reliable is the source?"

"It comes from an elf who was fired for shoddy workmanship on Barbie Dolls."

"All right, does anyone have any suggestions?"

Someone said, "Why don't we get someone to sprinkle his boots with depilatory powder, and then, when he puts them on, his beard will fall out? This will make him the laughingstock of the world."

"It's worth a try," said the chief. "What else?"

"How about smearing a chemical on his reins that would make him sick and lose control of his sled in flight?"

"You mean the stuff the plumbers were going to put on Jack Anderson's steering wheel?"

"It could work."

"Does Santa smoke cigars?"

"I don't know. Why do you ask?"

"We have some poison ones left over from the Castro caper."

"It's too complicated. This has to be simple, and we can't get involved directly in any way."

"What about putting out a contract on him through the Mafia? We could get Johnny Rossini to take a shot at him when he's making a drop in Chicago. Or Lucky Luchesi could have his boys waiting for him by his chimney in Detroit."

"I'll have to clear that with the director," the chief of the section said.

"How about his mail? Have we checked that out?"

"We've got three departments working on it full time. We've steamed open every letter going out to him."

"Suppose we slipped a ball-point pen containing a hypodermic needle with poison on it in one of the letters?"

"He might be wise to it. There has to be some way of getting to him without him knowing about it," the CIA chief said.

"Wait a minute. I think I've got it. Last year Santa Claus made a stop at a divorcée's house in Alexandria, Virginia. He stayed about an hour longer than he had to, and we taped what went on. It was pretty wild stuff. If the tape ever got out, it would destroy the old coot forever."

"So?"

"Why don't we take a page out of the FBI's book? We'll send Santa Claus the tape with an anonymous note. 'There are twenty-three days until Christmas. There is only one thing left for you to do. You know what it is. . . .'"

"I like it," said the chief. "It's clean and yet it's dirty. If that tape doesn't make him jump off the North Pole, nothing will."

Everyone in the room smiled and said, "Ho, ho, ho."

MAYBE EVERYONE IS CIA

In the early 1950s, thanks to Senator Joseph McCarthy, the words "commie," "pinko," and "red" were bandied about so freely that no one could be sure where anybody stood. It was a period of blacklisting, blackballing, and name-calling, the likes of which the country hadn't seen for a long time.

We are now going into a new phase of paranoia, and it has to do with the CIA hearings. Where once everyone was suspected of being either a member of the Communist

Party or a "fellow traveler," now everyone is accusing everyone else of working for the CIA.

The recent unsubstantiated and reckless charge that both Walter Cronkite and John Chancellor were reporting to the CIA is an example of how this country can go ape when it wants to.

My interest in the matter is very personal. As a friend of both Cronkite and Chancellor I am afraid that I also will be accused of working for the Central Intelligence Agency through guilt by association.

I wish to say for the record that although I have been to Chancellor's house for dinner and have spent time on Martha's Vineyard with Cronkite, playing tennis with him, I have never passed on any secrets from the Russians to either of them.

It isn't because they didn't try to get anything out of me. It was just that I was too smart to get caught in their web.

For example, I recall some time back seeing Chancellor at a party, and he said to me, "What do you think of Ford going to Vladivostok?"

"Why do you ask?" I said suspiciously.

"I'm going with him."

"Why would you go with him?" I asked.

"Well, as anchorman of the *NBC News* show I think I should."

What a beautiful cover, I thought to myself. Here was Chancellor going to Vladivostok ostensibly to cover President Ford's trip for NBC, when he probably was going to photograph the largest Soviet naval base in the Far East.

"I can't talk about Vladivostok," I said, not falling for his trap.

Later I heard Chancellor had told several people he thought I worked for the CIA because I wouldn't discuss Vladivostok with him.

I went to Tahiti a few years back with Cronkite, and

we visited Bora Bora, one of the most beautiful islands in the world.

One night I said to my wife, "Have you noticed how many pictures Walter's taking of the island?"

"What's wrong with that? Everyone's taking pictures. We'll probably never get to this place again."

"I know, but Walter's been taking them underwater."

"That's because he has an underwater camera."

"I wonder who gave it to him," I said.

When we got back to the United States I asked Walter if I could see his pictures, and he said, "Something happened to my camera, and most of them didn't come out."

The pieces started to fall into place, but I never said anything to anybody about it.

But I thought to myself, *Only the CIA would give someone a faulty underwater camera.*

It isn't just Chancellor or Cronkite. I've had suspicions about many other people whose behavior has been very strange. For example, who put up the money for Howard Cosell's live TV show from New York? Why did Barbara Walters go to China with Mrs. Ford? Who told Sally Quinn to quit the CBS morning show? Why does Joe Namath always call a girl from a different telephone booth? Doesn't it seem more than a coincidence that Bob Hope didn't go to Vietnam this Christmas?

These are tough times for all of us. Just the other day my wife bought a tiny Kodak Instamatic camera, the day after she sat next to George Bush at a dinner party. She said she wanted it to take pictures of the children. Maybe so, but I've decided it wouldn't hurt to tap her telephone line. When you live in a world where anything is possible a husband can't be too careful.

11

The Good Americans

MOTHER OF EXILES

The Statue of Liberty was gazing toward Europe when I tapped her on the shoulder. "Ma'am," I said, "if you look the other way, we have about one hundred and thirty thousand Vietnamese refugees coming in from Guam and the Philippines. I thought you might hold your torch high and light the way for them."

The statue seemed irritated. "We have too many people in this country now. What am I going to do with one hundred and thirty thousand Orientals?"

"The same thing you did with everybody else. Welcome them. They're tired, and they're poor, and they are yearning to breathe free."

"And what about jobs? Who is going to support them?" she said petulantly.

"You never worried about that before," I said. "Whoever came to this country eventually found jobs, and almost all of them made very good citizens. There is no reason to think the Vietnamese will be different. After all, you are the mother of exiles."

"Times have changed," she growled. "The American people aren't that thrilled about having a bunch of refugees dumped on them. Who is going to feed them? How many will go on welfare? How do we know their kids won't get in trouble in the streets? We have enough problems in this country without asking for more."

"But," I pleaded, "we're responsible for them being refugees. We screwed up a country like it's never been screwed up before. We supported their corrupt governments, loaded them down with weapons they couldn't use, defoliated their rice paddies, and wrecked their families.

"We left the country in a mess. The least we can do is take in whatever huddled masses escaped to our teeming shore."

"That's easy for you to say," the Statue of Liberty replied, "but we have to think of Americans first. They don't want any more foreigners in this country."

"But most of our fathers and grandfathers and great-grandfathers were foreigners. You've welcomed them all. Tell me the truth. Do you have anything against Orientals?"

"I don't personally. But you know how some people are. The Vietnamese have different habits, and they're from another culture. They just don't fit in. Besides, I'm supposed to welcome the homeless from Europe. That's why I'm looking in that direction."

"These people need refuge," I protested. "Their lives are in ruins. Remember when they flew in orphans from Vietnam and Cambodia? Nobody seemed to object to that."

"It's not the same thing," the statue said. "You can adopt orphans. But what can you do with refugees?"

"Help them find homes, jobs, make them citizens."

"It's out of the question. It isn't our fault they lost the war. Look, no one minds one or two Vietnamese in a community. But you're talking about thousands. They'll stick out like a sore thumb. The unions would never stand for it."

"Please don't turn your back on them," I begged. "If somebody just said, 'Welcome. We're glad you came,' most Americans would go along with it. The American people gripe a lot, but they'll do the right thing if somebody leads them. If you could shine your torch toward the Golden Gate Bridge, perhaps the people will be ashamed of the way they've behaved."

The Statue of Liberty turned slowly. There was a tear in her eye. "I've been here so long I amost forgot why I was holding this lamp. Where did you say I should shine my torch?"

"Over there. Hold it as high as you can and point it toward the West so every American can see it. That's it. Now repeat after me, 'Send these, the homeless, tempest-tossed to me, I lift my lamp beside the golden door.'"

VIETNAM NOSTALGIA

Henry Simpkin, who has a business called Nostalgia, Inc., called the other day and said, "We're bringing back the Vietnamese War."

"So early?" I said.

"It's the right time," he assured me. "People long for the good old days when we were fighting the Communist peril in the rice paddies of Asia. We need something to take our minds off inflation and recession. What better diversion than getting involved in Indochina again?"

"I don't know, Simpkin. Are you sure the American people want to be reminded of Vietnam so soon after we got out?"

"Listen, the President isn't asking for our boys to go back in again. All he wants is for Congress to allot hundreds of millions of dollars to help prevent the Vietcong from taking over the freedom-loving government of President Thieu."

"Do my ears deceive me?" I said. "I think President Ford is playing our song. It seems like only yesterday we were dancing to the same tune at President Johnson's Inaugural Ball."

"Of course, we'll have to send in advisers to help the South Vietnamese. But don't worry, the President has no intention of committing any American boys to fight a war six thousand miles away from home."

"Simpkin," I said, "I think you've got a hit. It's almost like being there again."

"Remember when we anchored the fleet off the Gulf of Tonkin and the North Vietnamese shot a torpedo at one of our destroyers?"

"How could I forget it?"

"Well, guess where I'm going to put the fleet now?"

"Off the coast of Indochina?"

"You better believe it. When you're going in for nostalgia, you have to be authentic or people won't buy the period."

"You've re-created the whole thing down to the naval task force," I told my friend in amazement.

"And I've got the Pentagon and White House lying again, just like the old days. They said we weren't flying any missions over Vietnam or Cambodia."

"It reminds me of the early sixties," I said.

"Guess what I'm also bringing back," Simpkin said.

"Bob Hope?"

"Better than Bob Hope. I'm bringing back dominoes."

"I almost forgot about dominoes!" I said excitedly.

"It was the most popular game during the Vietnamese war. You lined them up and if one went down, the next one fell and so on and so forth until they all fell."

"The old domino theory." I chuckled. "I have a box of them in the attic which I saved with my light at the end of the tunnel."

"This could be the biggest nostalgia kick the country has ever gone through," Simpkin told me. "We also hope to bring back the Ho Chi Minh Trail."

"The Ho Chi Minh Trail," I said, picking up my guitar and strumming the first few bars.

"And incursions and peace with honor and all the great

phrases that people used to love from the period. The President might even ask for a new draft, and then we'll organize demonstrations on the campuses. You can't have a nostalgic feeling about the war in Indochina without campus demonstrations."

"Simpkin, you've thought of everything."

"Do you know if we don't fight 'em in Vietnam, we'll be fighting them on the beaches of Hawaii?"

"I think so," I said. "Could you hum the first line and I'll pick it up on the chorus?"

THE GOOD AMERICANS

The hardest thing to find in Washington, D.C., these days is someone who was a hawk on Vietnam. Everyone you talk to was against the war from the start, and it's hard to imagine how we could have been there for fifteen years when so many people in power thought our involvement was such a big mistake.

"You know, I was always against the war," an aide in the Kennedy administration told me the other day.

"Oh," I said. "I thought you were for it."

"Publicly, I was for it," he said. "But privately I was against it. I worked behind the scenes to get us out of it. Ask my wife."

"I believe you," I said. "Why would you lie?"

When I got back to my office, I heard from one of President Johnson's national security advisers. "Well, I was right, wasn't I?"

"Right about what?"

"I said we couldn't win it with American troops. The Vietnamese people had to do it for themselves."

"But you told me in the sixties the pacification program was working and we were winning the war."

"I did not," he said angrily.

"Yes, you did. I remember you reading me the body

counts from Vietnam. You said I should believe you instead of the press reports coming out of there."

"I'm sure you got me mixed up with somebody else," he said nervously. "I was always suspicious of those body counts."

"Yeah," I said, getting him off the hook. "It must have been somebody else."

"Thanks," he said, "thanks a lot."

As luck would have it, I ran into a high CIA official on the street the next day. The last time I saw him was at a party where he said after a few drinks that anyone who didn't support the war in Vietnam was a traitor to the country. Someone took a poke at him, but the hostess broke up the fight before it really got started.

"I'm glad we're out of *that* one," he said, more friendly than I'd seen him in a long time.

"You are?" I said, rather surprised.

"The CIA knew it was hopeless from the beginning. It was the military that really screwed us up."

"I didn't know that," I said. "I thought the CIA played a big role in the war."

"Only to get us out. Our main thrust was to disengage from the war, but you know how generals are. They kept telling the President we could win it."

"I'm glad I ran into you," I said, "or I would have never known what the CIA was doing over there. It must have been a tough period for you, going to parties and getting into fights with people who were against the war."

"Yes, but that was my cover. I had to pretend I was a hawk when I really was a dove. I had everyone fooled."

"God bless you," I said. "No one would have ever guessed."

I went into the drugstore to buy some cigars and met a retired Air Force colonel I knew. "A CIA friend of mine just told me it was the military who kept us in Vietnam," I said.

"That's a crock," he said. "We always knew the bombing wouldn't work, but no one would listen to us. The politicians had no idea of what was going on over there. We carpet bombed that country from wall to wall, and they wouldn't give in. Someday, when the secret communiqués are released, you'll see that the military didn't want to have anything to do with that show."

When I got home, I found a letter from a former member of Henry Kissinger's staff, who wrote, "I had nothing to do with Vietnam. As a matter of fact, I kept four draft dodgers in my cellar all during the war so they wouldn't be shot. I was a good American."

THE YANKS ARE COMING?

"Mr. Secretary, Mr. Secretary."

"I'll take a question from the gentleman in the back of the room."

"Why is the United States sending fifty million in military equipment to Angola?"

"Because we are protecting the freedom-loving people of Angola against the aggression of Communists who are being supported by Soviet and Cuban arms. The security of the United States depends on an independent and neutral Angola."

"Why is that, Mr. Secretary?"

"Well, just look at this map. Here is the United States, and here is Angola. If Angola falls to the Communists, then the only thing that would separate us would be the Atlantic Ocean."

"Mr. Secretary, Mr. Secretary."

"The lady over there."

"How do we know the good Angolans from the bad Angolans?"

"By their names. The Popular Movement for the Liberation of Angola, egged on by the Kremlin, is trying to force its ideology on the National Front for the Liberation of Angola and the National Union for the Total Independence of Angola. The United States cannot sit idly by and see them swallowed up by the Popular Movement for the Liberation of Angola."

"In all due respect, Mr. Secretary, it's going to be very hard for the media to get Americans interested in this war when the names of the good guys and the bad guys are so hard to keep straight."

"I'm aware of that, and my people are working on it now. We were thinking of calling the Communist forces the Angola-Cong and the freedom fighters the Angola-Ese."

"And what will we hope to get out of supporting the Angola-Ese?"

"We hope to win the hearts and minds of the people through Angolanization. The President expects the Angolans to do their own fighting. All we intend to do is give them support and train them to defend themselves."

"Mr. Secretary, isn't that how we got into Vietnam?"

"I see no similarity between the Vietnamese war and the police action now raging in Angola. For one thing Angola is in Africa, and for another we have no intention of sending American boys six thousand miles to fight someone else's battles for them. All we are doing is giving the freedom-loving Angola-Ese the logistical support necessary to fight the Angola-Cong in the jungles of a former Portuguese colony."

"Would you consider using air power if the Angola-Cong refuse to stop their aggression?"

"Not before Christmas. But the President is keeping his options open. Luanda, which is now capital of the Communist forces, should realize that it is not immune to punishment if it does not respect the neutrality and independence of Angola."

"Mr. Secretary, what difference does it make whether the Popular Movement for the Liberation of Angola or the National Front for the Liberation of Angola or the National Union for the Total Independence of Angola rules the country?"

"It didn't make any difference until the Soviets started supporting the Popular Movement for the Liberation of Angola. Then we had no choice but to support the other two factions to uphold the spirit of détente."

"Mr. Secretary, what is our legal justification for getting involved in Angola?"

"Every President from Eisenhower on down has indicated the United States would never stand for a Communist presence in South-West Africa."

"When did Eisenhower say that, Mr. Secretary?"

"On June 12, 1956, John Foster Dulles warned President Eisenhower that if the Portuguese ever pulled out, there would be trouble in Angola. And do you know what Eisenhower said?"

"What did he say, Mr. Secretary?"

"He said, and it's in the files, 'Where the hell is Angola?' "

GIFT GIVING IN WASHINGTON

In years past gift giving between the President of the United States and a head of state was a simple matter. One of the President's staff would call up Tiffany's or Steuben Glass or Neiman-Marcus and ask them to select something appropriate for a foreign dignitary.

But those days seem to be gone, and now when a head of state comes to the White House, he expects a lot more.

Just the other day the president of Lovlost-by-the-Sea paid a state visit to Washington, and this was what transpired.

President Yak of Lovlost-by-the-Sea gave his gift first. "President Ford, on behalf of the citizens of Lovlost-by-the-Sea I present you this beautiful silk tie woven by one of our most famous weavers and sewn by hand by six virgins from the Calico Mountain area of my beautiful country. And for your lovely wife I present this beer mug which was made especially to celebrate the occasion of the tenth anniversary of our independence."

"Thank you very much, Mr. President. On behalf of the people of the United States I would like to give you a brand-new steel foundry which we shall finance for you."

"That's lovely, Mr. President. I also would like to present to you a book of proverbs written by our most famous poet, Lo Tak, before he was put under house arrest for attacking my government."

"Thank you, President Yak. And although I cannot present it to you personally, I want you to have as a token of our friendship a squadron of F-4 fighter planes which will be delivered to your country in the next six months."

"That is very kind of you, President Ford, and it brings tears to my eyes. In exchange, please accept this coconut, which, as you will notice, has a face carved on it that bears a great resemblance to me."

"I am overwhelmed, President Yak. Would you consider it out of line if I gave you three hundred heat-seeking missiles to go with your fighter planes?"

"You've given us so much already, but I would not insult you by refusing your wonderful gesture. I hope you will not be offended to accept, in exchange, this straw basket, which was made by one of our greatest artisans before he was shot for treason after the last coup d'état."

"A real straw basket! I shall build a special case for it. And now I have a surprise for you. Henry tells me you have your heart set on a nuclear energy plant."

"I told Henry it was just a dream."

"Well, we're going to make your dream come true. Just present this certificate to any U.S. nuclear energy company, and they will honor it."

"President Ford, what can I say? Would you accept

in exchange for it this elephant bracelet made by the widow of one of my former colonels in the army?"

"I've always wanted an elephant bracelet. Henry, is there anything else we can give President Yak?"

"You forgot the submarines, President Ford."

"Of course. President Yak, in honor of the long friendship between our two great countries we are presenting you with ten new submarines in any color you wish to choose."

"I shall tell my people that you are truly the greatest President the United States has ever had."

"There's just one more thing, President Yak. Why does your country always vote against the United States on every United Nations resolution?"

"Because, President Ford, we have no choice. We have to vote with our friends."

No News Is Good News

CASTING THE FIRST STONE

The CBS show *60 Minutes* raised an issue which people are still discussing in Washington. Should the media report on the private lives of public people? More specifically, should a politician's drinking and philandering be treated as news?

The doves in the press maintain that a politician should not be exposed for what he does after work, unless it interferes with his job.

The hawks say everything an elected official does is news, and the people should be informed as to his moral character from the day the person announces he is running for office.

Politicians are obviously on the side of the doves. In fact one congressman, let us call him Rawhide, said, "If we must answer to the people for our private lives, why doesn't the press answer for theirs? I'd like to know what Mike Wallace does with his evenings."

"I don't think you should take this personally, Congressman," I said.

"How do I know that Barbara Walters doesn't have a few belts before she goes on the *Today* show?"

"At six o'clock in the morning?" I asked in a shocked voice.

"Well, I think we should know as much about the people giving the news as we do about the politicans they report on."

"But that's ridiculous," I said. "I doubt if you could find a more clean-living group of professional men and women than we have in the media. Do you know what the White House correspondents do at night when they go on trips with the President?"

"What?" Rawhide asked.

"Needlepoint," I said. "They all make pillows for their wives."

"Have you actually seen them doing needlepoint?"

"No," I admitted, "but White House reporters never lie."

"I've heard lots of stories about newspapermen, but I've never repeated them on the floor of the House."

"It's good you didn't. You would probably be called on to back them up. Do you know how much Walter Cronkite or John Chancellor drinks?"

"Plenty, I'll bet," Rawhide said.

"One glass of wine with dinner, and only *after* they do the show. People in our profession realize that the youth of this country look up to us. We can't afford to have any scandal attached to our names."

"You're full of it," Rawhide said.

"Oh, on some special occasion such as New Year's Eve or VE-day, a journalist might let himself go and have two or three drinks. But I'll say this, Congressman, I never saw a drunk newspaperman I didn't like."

"Well, what about their sex lives? The FBI files are full of stories of newspapermen who were up to no good."

"Lies, all lies," I said. "Most newspapermen and television commentators have mothers whom they see every Sunday. Do you think they could face their mothers if they had anything to be ashamed of? Frankly, it might be better if members of my profession let their hair down every once in a while. But we just aren't built that way. We have a responsibility to our viewers, listeners, and reading public. And they expect each and every one of us to be Mr. Clean. How could we report on politicians if our hearts and minds were not pure?"

"I guess you're right," Congressman Rawhide said. "I'm sorry I raised the issue. Do you want to meet a beautiful secretary in my office?"

"I'd love to, sir. But I have to go to a prayer breakfast."

YOU ARE WHAT YOU EAT

There is good news for newspaper readers. Reports indicate that it may not be long before newsprint can be turned into food. A process now being developed involves extracting the glucose from the cellulose content of newsprint, then feeding the glucose to a batch of edible yeasts, molds or bacteria inside a fermenter. The protein left over would be dried into a powder and used as a nutrient supplement.

Dr. Barry Coombe of Australia has been feeding pellets made from newsprint to sheep, and he says they have been thriving on it.

This will, of course, present a new problem for the printed media. Not only will news reporters and columnists have to worry about how their words will affect the reading public, but they also will have to remember that people are going to eat them.

One question is: What news will be more digestible than others? Should you start the morning with a light breakfast of comics or a heavy breakfast of editorials? What wine do you serve with Jack Anderson's column, and would it be a mistake to eat the text of a Henry Kissinger press briefing before going to bed?

Dr. Coombe did not concern himself with the content

of the newsprint he fed his sheep, but I believe a lot more research has to be done before we permit human beings to eat their daily newspapers.

We do know that most people get indigestion when perusing their front pages. But we're not sure how their gastric juices would react if they started chewing on them.

Another question which would be raised is: If publishers discovered that there was money to be made from food in their paper, would they insist on their editors sugarcoating the news?

In a few years we could expect a series of cookbooks on how to prepare meals with your daily paper.

The recipes might go something like this.

"Chop up your newspaper until it is finely ground. Add three cups of water and mix into a paste. Then take a Dear Abby or Ann Landers column and separate the questions from the answers. Beat up the answers, and let them stand. Throw the questions away.

"Take a William Buckley column and let it simmer for fifteen minutes. Then add a dash of a President Ford speech (not much or your dish will be too bland), a pound of denials by the CIA, and season with a hot Herblock cartoon.

"Pour this into a pan, first greasing it with a full-page advertisement from one of the oil companies. Then add three strips of Peanuts and a Lou Harris poll.

"Stir the dish for twenty minutes. When it becomes a thick sauce, pour it over a leg of lamb which was fattened up by being put on a steady diet of pellets made from pictures of Jacqueline Onassis. The recipe should serve a family of four, but if you don't have enough sauce you can throw in Evans and Novak for gravy. The important thing is to serve before it gets too sticky."

The reason I have left myself out of the recipe is I am constantly hearing from readers who say that every time they read my column they throw up. If reading it can do this, we have to assume eating it could be very hazardous to your health.

THE STREETS OF SAN FRANCISCO

I have a problem and perhaps many other Americans are having it as well. I can't tell the TV news shows any more from the crime dramas that follow shortly afterward.

I'm not sure whether or not I saw Patty Hearst on Walter Cronkite or on *The Streets of San Francisco*. Was Sara Jane Moore a character in *Cannon,* or did she really try to shoot the President of the United States?

Reality and unreality blend into one. There doesn't seem to be much difference between the Lynette Fromme we see on *Eyewitness News* and the sick hippie we watch on *Hawaii Five-O*.

What do the crazy people do when they're not out in the streets aiming guns at people? Do they sit home and watch television? Do they fantasize that S.W.A.T. has their house surrounded or that the FBI's Efrem Zimbalist is hunting them in a helicopter?

Do they identify with the people who are trying to kill McCloud or the ones who are trying to rape Angie Dickinson in *Police Woman?*

When did John Chancellor go off the air and *Mod Squad* go on? There must have been a commercial break somewhere. Did I see a bank robbery on the six o'clock news, or was it on *Barbary Coast?* Was it the lady in *The Rookies* who had a .45 in her hand, or did I watch her on Harry Reasoner?

Who writes the news shows; who writes the crime dramas? Are they the same people?

Has President Ford seen too many John Wayne movies on TV?

I know I heard that a woman had her .44 taken away

from her and in twelve hours she was able to purchase a .38. But what show did I see it on? Was it the *Today* program or could it have been on *Baretta?*

Where are all the future Oswalds and the Arthur Bremmers now? Do they have color TV, or are they watching in black and white?

Was it Petrocelli, Ironside, Perry Mason, or Patty Hearst's lawyer I saw last night saying his client had been brainwashed?

They showed a gun on television that could shoot poison darts and kill someone in fifteen seconds. I think Dan Schorr talked about it—but then again it could have been on *Mission: Impossible.*

Did someone really try to kill Jack Anderson, or was it a man on *Conrack?* I wish I could recall.

There was a kidnapping on TV. I think it was a boy named Bronfman. They caught the kidnappers. Who did? The real FBI or was it Harry O? What shows do kidnappers watch after they're caught? The news programs or the crime dramas?

Are would-be killers jealous of Charles Manson? Do they envy Miss Fromme's TV exposure? Do they dream they will be the next ones grinning in the klieg lights that press against their police escorts?

Or do they pretend they're shooting it out with Charles Bronson on the ABC *Friday Night Movie.*

If I can't tell the real events from the fictional ones, how can they? Maybe there is no such thing as a real event anymore. Maybe there's no fiction. Then what is it we're watching, and what is it doing to us?

And if it's doing it to us, what is it doing to them—those lonely frustrated people sitting in their dingy rooms fondling the .22s, the .38s, and .45s and whatever else they bought in the store last week?

The National Rifle Association spokesman said on

Mike Wallace's show that guns don't kill people—people kill people. Or did I see that on *Kojak?*

For the life of me, I can't remember.

HEAT IN THE KITCHEN

One day shortly after Harry Truman took over as President of the United States, Bess Truman was cooking him some veal stew. It was summer, and unfortunately the air conditioning had gone out. Bess was irritable and yelled, "My it's hot in here." Harry, who also was irritable, yelled back, "If you can't stand the heat, get out of the kitchen."

Bess stomped out, and Harry went hungry that night.

I couldn't help thinking of Harry Truman's remark when I read about Ron Nessen's disenchantment with the press. When you think about White House news, you have to think about the kitchen.

Every day the President's press secretary is supposed to cook up news for forty or fifty regular White House reporters. In the days of Eisenhower, Kennedy, and even Johnson, the correspondents, with one or two exceptions, ate up everything that was served to them. Some of them wound up with indigestion. But they never complained because they were always hungry for news, and Jim Hagerty, Pierre Salinger, and Bill Moyers were able to whip up enough hash to satisfy them and their readers.

Then came Ron Ziegler. Although Ziegler was supposed to be the head chef, he never knew what Nixon's staff were cooking up in the kitchen. They would hand him a mess of pottage to take out to the press. "What is it?" he would ask, and they would tell him, "Steak."

Like a dummy, Ziegler would go out and tell the correspondents he was giving them Grade A certified beef.

For a while the reporters ate it. But then they started

getting stomach pains and complained to Ziegler that he was feeding them garbage.

This hurt Ziegler's professional pride, but everyone from President Nixon on down refused to change the menus. One day they sent out cornmeal, the next day dog food, and the third day thin gruel that had been condemned by the Food and Drug Administration.

"We can't live on this daily diet," the reporters screamed at Ziegler. "Give us something we can get our teeth into."

Ziegler ignored their pleas, and the daily feeding of the press became more and more acrimonious. Pretty soon the correspondents were throwing the stuff back in Ziegler's face, and he'd walk out of the press room with egg all over it.

Finally, the White House press corps decided to brown bag it and accept nothing the Nixon administration served up to them. As each White House cook was forced to resign, the heat in the kitchen got worse. In fact, it got so bad that even President Nixon decided he could not stand it and he got out for good.

So then came Ron Nessen. (Jerry terHorst made a few meals, but when he and President Ford could not agree on the ingredients of a briefing, he resigned.)

Nessen thought he could make the press briefings delicious occasions for everybody. He served up what he considered choice cuts of information and buttery items of news.

He was certain every time he threw the press a bone, they would believe it was a chicken. But unfortunately the White House correspondents had been burned by the Nixon administration and were still suspicious.

This lack of confidence seemed to be getting to Nessen. "I work day and night to feed them, and I get nothing but complaints. How can I cook up stories if they say I lied about the recipes?"

It's a good question that only a Harry Truman could answer.

And it stands now, every time Nessen comes out and says, "I have a juicy tidbit for all of you," some joker in the back always yells out, "I say it's spinach, and I say the hell with it."

THAT'S SHOW BIZ

There is so much bad news in the papers lately that when a bit of good news happens, we'll all grab it like a bobbing life preserver.

This year the news that seemed to warm everyone's heart was that CBS News had been conned out of $10,000 by a man who claimed to know where Jimmy Hoffa was (in a cement coffin twenty feet below the surface of the water off Key West, Florida).

CBS could have survived the financial loss without much difficulty, except that the New York *Times* got hold of the story and gave a detailed account as to how the network was taken. This embarrassed CBS no end because until then they hadn't considered the fact that being euchred out of $10,000 by a con man was a newsworthy event.

That evening after the network belatedly admitted it had been taken for a ride (to Key West of all places), a group of us were discussing why it gave us so much pleasure to read and hear about CBS' misfortune.

Each person in the room had his own ideas as to what really happened. This was mine.

Mike Wallace, Morely Safer, and Dan Rather of the *60 Minutes* are all dressed up in skin-diving suits and diving helmets ready to go over the side of the SS *Tipster,* which CBS has chartered to locate the most sought-after missing person in America.

Pacing the dock nervously are Don Hewitt, the producer of the show, and Richard Salant, president of CBS News.

Salant speaks to them. "Gentlemen, today you are going to make history. Through the miracle of electronic journalism we are going to raise Jimmy Hoffa from the depths of the waters off Key West. I have a map here which I bought from an old Cuban sailor in the bar, which shows the exact location of Hoffa's cement coffin. The sailor swore to me that the map has been in his family for six generations. He sold it to me for ten thousand dollars, which as you know is a steal. We are now anchored in the exact spot where the cross on the map is. Good luck and godspeed."

Wallace, Safer, and Rather are lowered into the water with a cameraman. Hewitt is manning the telephone. In ten minutes Wallace announces he's on the bottom. "Do you see the coffin?" Hewitt yells.

"No," says Wallace. "There's nothing down here but an old Spanish galleon loaded with gold coins and ingots of silver."

"Damn, we'll move a little north," Hewitt says. "Rather, do you see anything?"

"There's something here that looks like a coffin, but it's metal, not cement. I'll open it. . . ."

"Is it Hoffa?" Hewitt asks excitedly.

"No, it's just a bunch of old Aztec masks and Inca statues covered with diamonds, emeralds, and pearls. Should I bring them up?"

"Of course not. We have to find Hoffa. . . . Safer, where are you?" Hewitt is shouting.

"I'm about thirty feet from what looks like the treasure room of some sort of a pirate ship."

"Do you see any cement coffins?"

"Wait, I'm standing on one."

Salant grabs the telephone. "Is it Hoffa?"

"There's some writing on the coffin. I think I can make it out. It says, 'Judge Crater slept here.'"

"That does it," says Salant in disgust. "We were taken by a dirty old con man. Everybody come up."

Hewitt cries, "How could someone do this to CBS? We'll be the laughingstock of show business. What are we going to do for our show next Sunday?"

Salant says sheepishly. "Why don't we rerun the Haldeman interview?"

STORIES YOU WON'T SEE

If 1976 is anything like 1975, we can expect to see many wild newspaper stories. I can't tell you what they will be, but I can predict that these are the stories that you will *not* be reading in your papers next year.

TEHERAN, IRAN—The oil-producing countries meeting here today announced that they were lowering the price of oil by $4 a barrel. The shah of Iran told newspapermen, "We made a mistake when we raised the price of oil as it hurt the economies of most of the countries we deal with. To make it up to them, we plan to roll back prices to 1970. The goodwill of the world is more important to the oil countries than the few extra dollars that are at stake. We hope everyone will forget how in a weak moment we let greed get the best of us."

WASHINGTON—President Ford announced today he was going to take strong measures to turn around the economic slump in this country. He told reporters, "I've made up my mind and I've decided to take a stand. Government controls are the only answer to the problems we face. Appealing to the good sense of the American people is the stupidest thing any President could do."

NEW YORK—Muhammad Ali admitted to Howard Cosell on television last night that he wasn't the greatest fighter of all time or, for that matter, even now. "There are probably nine or ten heavyweights as good or better than I will ever be.

"I've been lucky during my career, but it can't last. There's something wrong with boxing when someone will pay a bum like me five million for one night's work. I'm just not worth it."

WASHINGTON—Nelson Rockefeller has applied for a loan from Bebe Rebozo to buy a home in Florida. Rockefeller said, "It was either getting the loan or having to sell my wife's jewels. As everyone knows, I'm not a rich man, and I don't think I've done anything wrong."

PARIS—The French government announced today that it was giving up its desire to be a world power and would take a backseat in any future international negotiations. A spokesman said, "The United States has always done what's best for France, and in the future, we'll let her speak for us on all substantive matters."

GENEVA, Switzerland—The price of gold dropped to $35 an ounce when world speculators bought Italian lire and English pounds instead. One banker said, "We consider the lira and the pound the two strongest currencies in Europe, and we don't want to be stuck with gold when they are revalued upward."

MOSCOW—Henry Kissinger told reporters today that he made a big mistake in his last negotiations with the Russians. "They really made a fool of me, and I'm walking away from this conference empty-handed. This isn't the first time it's been done to me. I guess my weakness is that I trust everyone I talk to. I should be more careful, but diplomacy really isn't my forte, and if I had to do it all over again, I would have stayed at Harvard."

WASHINGTON—George Meany of the AFL-CIO said at a dinner last night that one of the reasons for high prices was exorbitant labor demands that were preventing businesses from making a profit. "It is time," he said, "the unions worked harder and longer and stopped saying, 'Gimme, gimme, gimme.'"

NEW YORK—Walter Cronkite, last night on the

CBS News, did his show twice. Cronkite explained on the air that after he finished the first time and said, "And that's the way it is," he realized it wasn't that way at all, so he decided to do it again.

13

October Is for Poor People

AMERICA'S CHOICES

"Why," I cried the other night in despair, "out of a country of two hundred and forty million people can't we find an outstanding person to run for President?"

"It's very simple," said Turnbill, starting to write on a cocktail napkin. "There are one hundred and forty-four million people in the United States over eighteen who are eligible to vote."

"Right," I said.

"But at the moment there are only ninety-nine million registered voters."

"Well, you would still think that we could find one person in ninety-nine million."

Turnbill asked the waiter for another cocktail napkin.

"Out of this ninety-nine million, thirty-eight million are under thirty-five years of age and are, therefore, ineligible to run for the presidency."

"That probably eliminates a lot of good people," I admitted.

"Now one million were not born in this country, so they can't run either."

"That still leaves us with sixty million people to choose from."

"Wait," said Turnbill, starting on his third napkin. "About half of this number—thirty million, four hundred fifty-six thousand, seven hundred and eighty-two, to be exact, are women."

"So?"

"Well, you and I know the country isn't ready for a woman President for at least twenty years."

"That long?" I said in sorrow.

"Do you want facts or do you want to get sentimental?" he asked.

"Just give me the facts," I told him.

"This leaves us roughly twenty-nine million presidential prospects," he said.

"Even that's enough to find an outstanding man for President," I told Turnbill.

"But," he said, now writing on the tablecloth, "at least three million of the twenty-nine million have a fear of flying. You can't have a President of the United States who is afraid to fly. It would be a sign of weakness to our adversaries."

"All right, we're down to twenty-six million people to choose from."

Turnbill took out a pocket computer. "We have to take off two million because their wives don't want to move to Washington. Then there are two million more who are in some sort of trouble with the IRS and couldn't stand an audit."

"I must admit you're really cutting it down."

Turnbill kept hitting the keys of the computer. "Then there are twelve million who are just about to get a divorce or are living with someone in what Middle America still calls 'sin.'"

"I forgot about them."

"And you have to eliminate the gay people."

"You mean the country would never elect a gay person?"

"They won't even let one serve in the Air Force," Turnbill said.

"So where are we now?"

Turnbill kept hitting the computer. "We're down to nine million."

"That still is a lot to pick from."

"Not exactly. There are at least two million who could never pass an FBI security check because they belonged to some left-wing organization or were involved some way with Watergate."

"All right, so you have seven million left. Can't we find one good man in seven million?"

"We could except that the country will never accept a President who has had a mental disorder or has been treated by a psychiatrist."

"And seven million people in this country have been treated by psychiatrists?" I asked.

"Not seven million," Turnbill said. "There have been only six million, nine hundred and ninety-nine thousand, nine hundred and eighty-seven who have had psychiatric treatment."

"So that leaves us with Ford, Reagan, Humphrey, Wallace, Carter, Jackson, Bentsen, Bayh, Shapp, Udall, Harris, Sanford, and Shriver," I said.

Turnbill rechecked his figures. "That's all there is. I'm sorry about that."

"Don't be sorry," I told Turnbill. "At least you're the first guy who ever explained it to me."

OCTOBER IS FOR POOR PEOPLE

"October," my friend Sedgewicke told me as we sat on a street curb, "is absolutely the best month for poor people."

"How's that?" I asked him.

"It's just before election time, and all the politicians need us. Everyone promises that if he is elected, he's going to do something for the poor. Of course, they don't, but it gives you a real warm feeling to hear everyone talking about you. Do you know that I've shaken hands with three congressional candidates, had my picture taken with an incumbent mayor, been interviewed on television with a guy running for governor, and they told me if I sit here today, I might wind up in a TV commercial for a senator up for reelection?"

"Doesn't it get you angry that they use you just for election purposes?"

"I should say not," Sedgewicke replied. "I don't have anything to do and, I'll be honest with you, I like the excitement of a political campaign. A lot of poor people resent politicians coming into the neighborhood just before election time with their campaign managers and busloads of press. But I don't feel that way. I figure we're a very important part of the democratic process. If it weren't for us, politicians would have a tough time getting on TV. Have you ever seen a candidate talking to a rich person on television?"

"I must say, Sedgewicke, you have a good attitude. If I were poor, I would be very bitter about the politicians in this country."

"What is there to be bitter about?" Sedgewicke said. "If it weren't for poor people, the rest of the country wouldn't know how well off they were. No matter how bad things get, the politicians can always point to us and say that a majority of the people in this country really have never had it so good. Would you like a piece of my stale roll?"

"No, thank you, Sedgewicke."

"The only thing that disturbs me," he said, "is that there are a lot more poor people now, and we're not as much a novelty as we were in previous elections. They also have us broken down in categories. Before if you were poor—you were just poor. Now you're competing with people who are 'economically disadvantaged,' 'culturally deprived,' 'senior citizens,' and 'oppressed minorities.' Just yesterday a guy running for police chief came in the neighborhood, and I was about to shake hands with him for a TV station when his press representative pushed me aside and said they wanted the candidate to be filmed shaking hands with a black. Now I have nothing against blacks, but I don't think they should get priority when it comes to having their pictures taken with a guy running for chief of police. That's what you call poverty discrimination."

As we were talking, we heard a loudspeaker on a car. "Here comes the senator," Sedgewicke said as he got up and brushed himself off. "Well, I've got to go to work."

"How do you know he'll stop here?" I asked.

"It's in front of a supermarket. All the candidates are doing supermarkets this year."

Sure enough, the car stopped right in front of us, and the candidate got out.

"Aren't you going to shake hands with him?" I whispered.

"Not until the TV guys are set up," Sedgewicke replied. "Most poor people don't have enough sense to wait until the press get out of their bus. Okay, they're ready now. SENATOR, WHAT ARE YOU GOING TO DO ABOUT US POOR PEOPLE?" Sedgewicke shouted.

The senator put his arm around Sedgewicke and looked into the cameras, "I'm glad you asked me that. As you know, I have always been concerned about the cruel poverty in this great country of ours and. . . ."

I started to walk away, and Sedgewicke, grinning, yelled after me, "Don't forget to watch the six o'clock news."

TALKING TO THE LOSER

In every political contest there is a winner and a loser. You hear a lot from the winner but nothing from the loser. What happens to a defeated candidate? How does he feel?

"Governor Habadasher," I said.

"Oh, you still remember me?" Habadasher smiled.

"You only lost the election Tuesday, Governor."

"People forget fast in this state, son."

"It must be tough to have been a governor and then be turned out by the people. What was the first thought that came to your mind when they told you that you had lost the election?"

"I thought about all the good things I had hoped to accomplish for this state—the unfinished business that I had started, the dreams that were shattered by an electorate that didn't understand what I was trying to do."

"That's very nice, Governor. But what were you *really* thinking?"

"Well, if you want me to level with you, the first thought that came to mind was 'Damn, there goes my helicopter.' You know, I really got to love that helicopter. It would land right out there on the front lawn and zoom! I was above all the traffic and the stinking congestion and lousy air down there, and I could get to the football game in fifteen minutes. There's no feeling like it."

"No one could fault you for thinking that. Do you blame anyone for losing the election?"

"I blame myself, only myself. Of course, I had lousy TV commercials. I mean they really stank. But every time I complained they told me I didn't know anything about show business. And those infantile newspaper ads didn't help me any, nor did my campaign staff who seemed to be drunk every time I needed them. And I'll tell you this—I got creamed because some idiot was running for senator on the same ticket as I was, and his opponent stole all my votes. Except for that, I would say it was my fault."

"That's very generous of you, Governor. Your wife said after your defeat that she was happy you were getting out of politics."

"She was lying. She enjoyed being the governor's wife more than I enjoyed being governor. Boy, did she love all those servants and that chauffeured limousine and everyone playing up to her because she lived in the mansion. She may have told the press she was happy I was getting out of politics, but she hasn't talked to me since I lost the election."

"Governor, what does the future hold for somebody like you? Where does one go after being the head of a state?"

"I'd like to get into the Cabinet."

"President Ford's Cabinet?"

"Why not? He blew the election for me with his pardon. The least he could do is give me a Cabinet post."

"But if he gave everyone who lost the election a high post in his administration, the President would have to hold his Cabinet meetings in RFK Stadium."

"That's what my wife said."

"Governor, by American standards, you're a loser. You have tasted the bitter fruit of defeat. Having lived through it, would you advise young people to run for public office?"

"I certainly would."

"Why?"

"Because if you win, you have a chance of getting your own helicopter. There's nothing like it, son. You're flying way up there in the clouds, and when you look down, all you see are suckers jammed bumper to bumper trying to get home from the football game."

BREAKING THE TAX CODE

Deep in the bowels of the Internal Revenue Service building is a large steel door with a sign outside of it which says RESTRICTED AREA—AUTHORIZED PERSONNEL ONLY.

Two armed guards are stationed in front of it, and everyone who goes in and out is checked twice. This special bureau, called FITF, is in charge of devising federal income tax forms that no one can understand. A staff of cryptographers and code experts work day and night to devise new methods of foxing the taxpayer so he will be unable to fill out his 1040 form.

Last May an IRS agent in the Minneapolis office started to go over the 1974 return of a soybean farmer in Duluth when he sat up with a start. The form had been filled out by the farmer himself, and there were no mistakes.

He immediately picked up his phone and called the director of FITF.

"Sir," the agent said, "I think someone has broken our 1040 Code. I have a soybean farmer in Duluth who filled out his tax return without the aid of an accountant or a tax lawyer."

"Are you sure it just wasn't an accident?" the director said.

"Certain, sir. He was even able to fill out Part III 16 B which refers to Section D Lines 12 (a) and 14 (c) by combining the amounts shown on line 5 and 13."

"Oh, my God," the director said. "Did he get Part V Question 40 by reducing his gain on line 18 to the extent of the loss, if any, on line 39, as referred to in Instruction K?"

"Perfectly, sir. It's as if he had our code book in front of him while he was filling out the form."

"I'll notify the commissioner and secretary of the treasury at once." The director hung up and picked up his red hot-line phone.

An hour later a group of grim-faced people were sitting in the office of the secretary of the treasury, who was pacing up and down. "How did it happen?" he shouted at the commissioner of internal revenue. "You promised me that no one would be able to make head or tail of the 1974 return."

The commissioner looked angrily at the director of FITF. "What happened, Mulligan?"

"I don't know," said Mulligan. "Maybe the soybean

farmer is some kind of mathematical nut. We tried the 1974 form out on ten thousand people, including a thousand IRS agents, and not one of them understood it. It seemed foolproof."

The secretary of the treasury walked over to his window. "Do you know what this means? If a soybean farmer in Duluth has the key to our 1040 returns, that means other people will soon have it. We'll have millions of people filling out their own income tax forms. It could destroy every tax law and accounting office in the country."

The commissioner said, "It looks like we have no choice. We're going to have to change the 1040 form and make it so complicated that even H & R Block won't understand it. Can you do it, Mulligan?"

"Yes, sir," Mulligan replied. "But I'll need more people."

"Take anyone you want," the secretary of the treasury said. "This has highest priority. The very fabric of the American tax system is at stake. I want daily reports on your progress. I want that form to look like the greatest bunch of gobbledygook anyone has ever read."

The commissioner said, "We'll do it, sir. By the time the new returns are sent out there won't be five people in the country who will know how to fill it out."

"Not five people!" the secretary said. "I don't want anybody to understand it, including myself."

Mulligan replied, "Don't worry, Mr. Secretary. When my people get finished with it, the American taxpayer won't even be able to find the right line for his name and address."

The rest is history. As everyone who received his 1040 Tax Form for 1975 knows, FITF came up with a return that defied imagination. The secretary was so pleased he presented Mulligan with the U.S. Medal of Bureaucratic Balderdash with an Oak Leaf Cluster, the highest award the tax agency can bestow on an IRS employee in peace-time.

THE ANSWER TO CRIME

Howard Anderson of Cambridge, Massachusetts, has just come up with the ultimate solution to violent crime. The answer is "nonviolent crime." The problem as Howard sees it is that society expects people who commit street crimes to completely reform and after their punishment commit no crimes at all.

"This is impossible," he said, "and can't work. The statistics show that the majority of criminals go back to committing street crimes again and again because our present prisoner reform does not work."

Anderson's plan is this. Instead of prisons teaching inmates so-called honest trades, a program should be initiated to teach them white-collar crimes, which pay so much better and don't seem to get anyone in the United States too upset.

The idea would be for the Harvard Business School, the Wharton School of Business at the University of Pennsylvania, the Yale Law School, and other institutions of higher learning to set up courses in state and federal prisons where criminals could be taught the skills of committing white-collar crimes.

The curriculum would include accounting, banking, stock market fraud, bribery, kickbacks, and embezzlement. The teachers would explain the advantages of white-collar crime over street crimes. The average take for a street crime in the United States is $9.75. For the work and risk involved it hardly pays at all.

There are other disadvantages.

When a person gets caught committing a street crime, he usually winds up with some court-appointed lawyer who couldn't care less if the defendant gets twenty years or life.

A criminal who commits a street crime is treated with contempt by the police and society in general. In fact, the smaller the take, the less respect the criminal engenders from the judge and the jury and, therefore, the heavier the sentence.

But white-collar criminals have the opposite effect on everyone. A man who has embezzled a million dollars from widows and orphans is one to be looked up to and respected.

An officer of a large corporation who is involved in stock fraud is considered a pillar of his community and can get hundreds of people to testify to his good character.

A president of a bank who steals his depositors' money is usually forgiven by everyone *before* the trial.

A politician who has been arrested for accepting bribes or selling judgeships is always addressed as "sir" by the police.

The people in jails could be persuaded that the same amount of time it takes to mug an old lady in the park could be spent arranging for a municipal contract to be given to a corrupt builder or a bribe-paying road contractor.

To convince them, the course would include lectures by judges who could describe the lightness of sentences meted out to white-collar criminals. Bus tours could be arranged to "open-air" prisons where white-collar criminals are sent for punishment.

There would be lectures by ex-white-collar cons on how to seek the best legal advice after they are caught.

The beauty of Anderson's plan is that it does not ask a criminal to give up his trade. All it does is teach the convict socially acceptable methods of committing crimes that do not annoy the public.

When the average street crime convict discovers how

much money there is in white-collar crime and how little risk there is in getting punished, we can expect a dramatic drop in street crime, which is the only type that seems to shake anyone up in this country.

SARA LEE FOR SENATE

"Rep. Bella Abzug said last week that the recent Supreme Court ruling on campaign expenditures would make it harder than ever for women to run for public office.

"The reason, she said, is that most women candidates simply do not have ties to multimillionaires who can put unlimited amounts of money into political advertising under the court's decision."—New York *Times* item.

What Ms. Abzug says is probably true. But there is a certain type of woman who does have access to multimillionaires and who might decide to run for public office.

The scene is an apartment on Park Avenue. Huddleston Threabody III has just arrived.

"Sara Lee. Where's my little cheesecake hiding?" he yells.

"Here I am, Tiger," says Sara Lee, running out in her black negligee and throwing her arms around him. "Did my Tiger have a tough day at the office?"

"Tiger had a marvelous day. The stock market went up twenty points. The reason I'm late is that I stopped by Tiffany's and bought my little Sara Lee a present." He hands her a box.

She opens it and takes out a diamond bracelet.

"It's very nice," she says.

"Nice? It cost me a bundle. Don't you like it?"

Sara Lee takes Huddleston over to the couch and cuddles up to him. "I don't want jewelry anymore."

"A fur coat then! Go to Bergdorf's tomorrow and pick up a fur coat. Anything my little cheesecake wants."

"I don't want a fur coat. I have five already," she says, chewing on his ear.

"A trip? Would you like to go to Paris? I'll say I have to go to Europe for the firm."

"No, I don't want to go on a trip."

"Well, what do you want?"

Sara Lee, as she unbuttons Huddleston's shirt, says, "I want to run for the Senate from New York."

"You want to do what?"

"I want to run for the Senate. It would be a lot of fun, and it's something that would make me think of you all the time. Is my big strong Tiger going to let me run?"

"Now wait. Diamonds and fur coats are one thing, but financing a Senate campaign is another."

"I'll bet if that skeleton wife of yours wanted to run for the Senate, you'd give her the money," Sara Lee pouts.

"That isn't true. I'm not sure I want to put up money for anyone running for public office. Look, how would you like a new Aston-Martin to go with your Mercedes-Benz 450?"

Sara Lee moves to the other end of the couch. "I don't want another car. I want to serve my country. If you really cared for me, you'd let me announce my candidacy."

"I love you," Huddleston protests. "I'd do anything for you. But if I give you the money to run for public office, I'm going to have to declare it. My wife is going to ask me why I'm supporting you. Where are you going?"

"I'm getting into something *less* comfortable."

"Little cheesecake,"—Huddleston jumps up, trying to grab her—"would you like a town house instead of an apartment?"

"Unhand me, you brute." Sara Lee pushes him away. "I've never asked you for a thing, and finally, when all I want for my itty-bitty self is a chance to run for the Senate, you say I can't do it. Well, find someone else who is more interested in jewels than politics. I'm changing the lock on my apartment door."

"Baby, baby," Huddleston says in a lather. "Don't do this to me. I can't live without you. You don't know what these Wednesday evenings mean to me."

"If you feel that way, then I would think you'd like to prove it with something tangible. How are we women ever going to get elected if our gentlemen friends don't give us the money?"

"All right, all right. How do I make out the check?"

Sara Lee throws her arms around him. "Just make it out to the 'Sara Lee for Senate Committee.' Oh, Tiger, you're a living doll. Let's go into the bedroom and talk about my campaign."

14

Hail to the Chief

AN OFFICIAL SLOGAN FOR THE U.S.

My colleague Jack Anderson has been running a slogan contest for the Bicentennial. He is offering all sorts of prizes to the person who will come up with the words that will describe this country the best.

I was thinking of entering the contest, but I knew I couldn't win because people would think it was a put-up job. Since I hate to see my slogan go to waste, I have decided to use my own column to publicize it.

I believe the slogan that describes this country the best is "The check is in the mail."

My reason for selecting it as the best one is that it is easy to remember, it fits on automobile bumper stickers, and millions of Americans have been using it for years.

I must admit the slogan isn't original with me. I first heard my father use it forty years ago. In fact, every time the phone rang at our house he would say it to the caller on the other end.

One time I asked him after a call from the electric company if the check was really in the mail and he said, "Don't ask such dumb questions. If the check was in the mail, you wouldn't be eating meatballs and spaghetti tonight."

My father must have told other people about it because in no time at all I kept hearing the phrase being repeated wherever I went.

Most companies would blow their minds when they were told by a customer that "the check was in the mail." But there was little they could do about it.

Then one day a comptroller of a large corporation got a brainstorm. Why couldn't his company tell another company the same thing? In that way his company could slow up payments on its bills and use the money itself. He tried it and improved the cash position of his company by 100 percent.

Pretty soon everyone doing business was assuring everyone else that "the check was in the mail," and it took weeks, even months before anyone was paid.

The practice might have been stopped except that the people telling the tale got help from an unexpected source —the U.S. Post Office.

As time went on, postal service got so bad in the country that no one could tell if the person who said the check was in the mail was lying or not. Today it's impossible for anyone to know if the debtor is telling an untruth or if the check is really lost somewhere in a mailbag between St. Louis, Missouri, and Butte, Montana.

This has encouraged almost everyone in the country to blame the mails for the lack of payment of a bill.

For a long time only individuals and private enterprise used the ploy. But recently the government has gotten into the act. Now, whether you're waiting for a Social Security check or payment for a highway contract, there is someone in Washington who will tell you in a friendly voice that "the check is in the mail." It wouldn't be so bad if it was a real person, but most government departments are now using taped recordings.

A recent Gallup Poll showed that more people in the United States say, "The check is in the mail," than "Have a nice day."

It has become so much a part of our culture that it

should become the national slogan, replacing "In God We Trust." The American people have discovered that putting their trust in God is no assurance that anyone is going to get paid.

I want no prizes for my slogan. But if we adopt it officially, I hope my father will get the credit in our history books as being the first American ever to use it. Little did he know in those dark days of the Depression that someday his words would be on the lips of every man, woman, and college student in this country.

OVER THERE, OVER THERE!

LONDON—It seems only fitting that during the celebration of our Bicentennial we visit the mother country to which all of us owe so much.

I am happy to report, with only a few exceptions, that most Englishmen have gotten over the American Revolutionary War. In a few of the private gentlemen's clubs in London you may still hear someone shout, "We've got to send more military aid to the Tories in the colonies!"

But now these men are, thankfully, in the minority, and most of the British people are willing to write off the Revolution as a bad show that George III got them into by duplicity and overconfidence.

Still, one hard liner at White's Club told me, "We should have never gone in there with the Hessians unless we expected to win. Our problem was we didn't use everything in our arsenal against the revolutionaries. The only thing those shifty-eyed colonialists understand is force."

"Do you blame George the Third for getting you into the war you couldn't win?"

"I blame the War Office. They never understood the terrain, and they didn't think the insurrectionists would fight. After all, they reasoned, how could a rabble of uncivilized frontiersmen face up to the superior quality of arms and training of His Majesty's troops? But we still could have won if Parliament had not tied George the Third's hands when it came to voting more aid."

There is also still a great deal of criticism in some circles of the military. At Boodle's Club a retired major told me, "If General Wolfe had not been killed at Quebec in 1759, we never would have lost. He was the only military leader we had. In London Lord North received so many optimistic reports from the likes of General Howe and Sir Henry Clinton that we all thought His Majesty's boys would be home by Christmas. We were lulled into a false sense of security by General Cornwallis' extremely inflated body counts. Everyone over there insisted Washington was finished at Trenton, New Jersey."

Another hawk on the colonies, Colonel Blaime, Ret., said, "I don't know whether to say this publicly or not, but the reason we lost is the navy. Admiral Graves' decision not to engage the French off the Chesapeake Bay was a disaster. I'm still waiting for an inquiry, but I doubt if it will take place. Too many heads would roll."

Although the war is still being fought at White's and Boodle's, the man in the street rarely thinks about the American Revolution anymore. The consensus among most Britishers is that it's over and done with and England may be a better place for having given the colonialists their independence.

"I was for us being there at the beginning," an old man in Hyde Park told me. "But then they invented television, and when I saw with my own eyes the frightful atrocities being committed by British troops, I changed my mind."

An English banker said he was glad the American war was over because it had been such a drain on the budget.

"We never really needed the colonies," he said. "I would hate to think of what this country would be like today if America was part of the Empire. The pound would be weak, and we'd have to defend the dollar. We would be obliged to teach the natives everything from labor negotiating to productivity. Heaven knows how long it would have taken the colonies to get their economy in order and bring their standard of living up to ours. Besides, you could never trust an American to remain a loyal subject of the Crown."

"Why do you say that?" I asked him.

"Just look at what your people did to Nixon."

HAIL TO THE CHIEF

The American Indians seem to be divided over whether or not to participate in the Bicentennial celebration next year. Some tribes are going along with the festivities because they have decided it's good for their jewelry business. But others are boycotting them on the grounds that the Indians really have nothing to celebrate.

Chief Hard Nose of the Kalorama Indians, whose forefathers once hunted buffalo and bear where the Watergate now stands, told me his people have no interest in celebrating the two hundredth anniversary of the United States.

"Why should we celebrate an anniversary that was the start of us losing everything on this continent?"

"How can you say that?" I asked. "You've got a Bureau of Indian Affairs."

"Before you people formed a country, we had clean air, fresh water, and blue skies. And we had an ozone layer to keep us from getting skin cancer. Now you've messed things up so badly it isn't even safe to eat chicken eggs."

"But, Chief, look what we gave to your continent: railroads, highways, suburbs, shopping centers, and trading stamps. Where would the American Indian be today without the white man?"

"We'd be living in Palm Springs, Miami, and Beverly Hills."

"Ah, but what kind of life would you be living?" I asked. "You'd still be in tents, sleeping on buffalo hides and fishing in streams and dancing around fires. What type of existence is that?"

"It's better than selling souvenirs on the rim of the Grand Canyon," Chief Hard Nose said. "Frankly, I don't know what you people are celebrating anyway. Look what you've done to New York! When we sold you Manhattan Island for twenty-four dollars, New York bonds were worth their weight in beads. Every tribe with a pension fund fought to buy them. Now you can't give them away.

"When the settlers first arrived, there were trees and hills and streams from Wall Street up to Columbia University. You could ride a horse from the Hudson River to the East River in ten minutes. Now it takes an hour to get from First Avenue to the West Side Highway. What kind of progress is that?"

"New York isn't America," I pointed out to Chief Hard Nose. "Look at Detroit and Newark and Wilmington, Delaware. The Indians never could have developed those places on their own. When we celebrate our two hundredth anniversary, we're celebrating it for all Americans, and that includes you Indians. We couldn't have made it without you."

"Why do you say that?"

"Don't forget it was on your land that we found the gas and oil and coal and from that made this country what it is today."

"Then how come we don't get anything out of it?"

"Because we know you are a proud people who would never accept money for land that was stolen from you."

Chief Hard Nose said, "Why don't you try us?"

"We must forget the past," I told him. "Your people and our people must join hands and rejoice in this great

Bicentennial celebration. You are part of our culture. Without Indians there might never have been a movie industry or John Wayne."

"I forgot about John Wayne," he admitted.

"And don't forget your people gave us the names for three professional football teams. No other ethnic group has been so honored."

Chief Hard Nose thought for a moment and then said, "If we join in your Bicentennial, will you honor the treaties and promises you made to us for the last two hundred years?"

"Of course," I promised. "Have we ever lied to you?"

15

Come and Get Me, Copper

THE BIG ISSUE

The difference between this year and last year on Martha's Vineyard was that last year we all were talking about Nixon's resignation and this year we were talking about whether Susan Ford should have an affair or not.

The island is about equally divided on the issue. The Up-Islanders believe Mrs. Ford did the right thing when she said on television that premarital relations with the right person might help lower the divorce rate.

The Down-Islanders were shocked and felt that as First Lady it was Mrs. Ford's duty to speak out against pillowing before one got married.

MacIntosh, my tennis partner, thought Mrs. Ford purposely said what she did to guarantee that Susan would not have an affair.

"What do you mean?" I asked.

"Well, after all this publicity, Susan Ford is the only girl in America who doesn't have a chance of having an affair with *anybody*. The whole world is watching her now, and she can't make a false move."

"My gosh," I said, "I never thought of that. Mrs. Ford knew exactly what she was doing when she spoke out for premarital relations. Poor Susan. No guy will make a move."

"I wish I had thought of it," MacIntosh said. "I've got

an eighteen-year-old daughter, and the public couldn't care less what she does."

"The same with my daughter," I said. "I don't have one Secret Service man to watch her when she goes out on a date. Susan has at least a dozen."

"If Ford gets elected in '76," MacIntosh said, "Susan won't be able to go to a drive-in movie with a guy alone until she's twenty-one."

"And if Ford gets reelected in '80, Susan will be watched night and day until she's twenty-four," I said.

"Then it really doesn't matter whether she has an affair or not," MacIntosh said. "If she isn't married by then, most people will feel she's entitled."

"Why do you think people got so mad at Mrs. Ford for saying she wouldn't be upset if Susan told her she was having an affair?"

"Most of the people who got angry know they have no control over what their kids do, and they were mad that the wife of the President said it out loud."

"I'm glad she said it," I admitted. "I knew where Jerry Ford stood on oil, the Middle East, and New York City, but there was always that lingering doubt in my mind about where Mrs. Ford stood on premarital bundling. It's healthy to have a First Lady who tells it as it is."

"I wish Mrs. MacIntosh saw it that way," MacIntosh said. "Whenever my daughter goes out with one of the great unwashed, my wife goes up the wall."

"Is she afraid your daughter is going to have sex?"

"No," said MacIntosh. "She's afraid our kid is going to get cholera."

"I dig," I said.

"I wonder if it will hurt Ford's chances in the election?"

"Your daughter getting cholera?"

"No," said MacIntosh. "Mrs. Ford saying she wouldn't kick Susan out of the White House if she admitted to having an affair."

"It won't unless the Democrats make something of it."

"How could they do that?" MacIntosh asked.

"They could put out bumper stickers which read, 'Can Susan Ford chew gum and smooch at the same time?'"

JUST PLAIN FOLK

I watched Barbra Streisand on a TV special from Kennedy Center where she sang at a benefit for the Special Olympics for the Mentally Retarded.

She received a tremendous ovation after one of her songs, and she said she was surprised because she thought people in Washington were "stuffy."

It occurred to me that Miss Streisand was speaking for many Americans who somehow think that those of us who live in the nation's capital are different from other people in the country.

Well, it's not true. We're just simple folk with the same dreams and aspirations as everyone else. In the morning we insert our legs in our pants, one at a time, just as men and women do in Topeka and Peoria. And after a breakfast quite similar to ones eaten all over America, we go to our offices where we do our simple work.

The work is no different from that done in Hartford, Connecticut, or Atlanta, Georgia. Some of us will pass laws, others will filibuster, and still others will read Bella Abzug's mail. One man in a small office might give a squadron of jets to an Arab country, and another man in a small office will send missiles to Israel.

We could give a billion dollars to the space program or cut $500,000,000 to education. We'll tap telephones if we have to and add to files of suspected subversives.

Some people might be assigned to following Russian

diplomats all over town, and others could be in charge of selling them wheat.

We might work on ways of giving the American people a tax cut or figure out methods of bailing large corporations out of debt.

Some of us will lunch with lobbyists, while a few will eat with their secretaries and take the afternoon off.

People should stop thinking just because we live in Washington we're different.

We indict attorneys general and White House aides, pardon previous presidents, defend multimillion-dollar antitrust suits, and try to get government agencies off our clients' backs.

We cut food stamp aid, raise Social Security rates, and declare budget deficits. Some of us lie to grand juries, and others lie to Senate committees. We make speeches for TV audiences and hand out press releases telling how wonderful we are.

Some of us work for the media, and no matter what we say, we're always right.

We're a typical community. After work we may go over and have a few drinks with the ambassador of Iran or play a game of tennis with the secretary of the treasury. On some nights we might go to have dinner with the Fords, and on other evenings we'll have the Kissingers in for bridge and a light buffet.

If the weather is good, we could have a cookout at the Tidal Basin or wander down to the local tavern and have a few beers with Nelson Rockefeller. If there is a good movie in town and Barbra Streisand is singing beforehand, we might even go to that. Otherwise, we'll stay at home and read the *Congressional Record*.

It's sad that although we live in Washington, people think we're something special. We're just average Joes, a little better educated, more informed, rarely in error, and confident that nobody knows better than we do what's good for the country. How could Barbra Streisand think we're stuffy?

GUNS OF AUTUMN

I'd never seen Remington, my gun-loving friend, so angry.

"Did you see that show they did on CBS called the *Guns of Autumn* about hunting in the United States?"

"Yes, I did and it left a deep impression on me," I said. "The thought of those helpless hunters setting out to shoot ferocious deer and man-eating rabbits was almost too much to bear. I was on the side of the hunter. All he had to protect himself with was a shotgun or a rifle, while the animals had the protection of their speed, their claws, their teeth, and their intimate knowledge of the forest. You would think a country as great as ours would find ways of killing animals without stacking the odds against the poor guy with a gun."

Remington said, "The show made us look like damn fools. They showed all the worst aspects of hunting animals and none of the good things that go with the sport."

"I noticed that," I agreed. "It seems to me CBS went out of its way to depict how cruel game shooting was. I wrote them a letter and told them I thought that if they show what a man can do to a bear, they should also show what a bear can do to a man. It would have been much more balanced if there were a few scenes showing a bear tearing a hunter limb from limb. I would have enjoyed that."

"Well, we fixed them," Remington said. "We scared every advertiser from sponsoring the show. When you mess with the hunters in America, you're messing with the National Rifle Association. And when they start putting pressure on advertisers, there isn't a company in the United States that will defy the gun lobby."

"Thank God for the NRA," I said. "If it weren't for

their members, you would now have buffalo herds grazing on Fifth Avenue."

"What got me," said Remington, "was how biased the documentary was. They didn't show any of the pleasure people get out of hunting—the camaraderie and fellowship that the sport produces, the joy of walking in the woods early in the morning stalking an elk or sitting in a blind waiting to blast away at a flock of ducks. That's what hunting is all about. All they emphasized was the slaughter of the birds and animals. I don't call that balanced journalism."

"It isn't," I assured Remington. "If I were doing such a show, I would film the human side of hunting. I would show the love of man for his gun, a love greater than he has for even his own family. I would depict the sacrifices a hunter has to make to pursue this age-old sport where a man must pit his wits against the wiliest animals in the forest. I would show the patience and perseverance that it takes to shoot just one pheasant in the back or one doe in the head. What people don't realize who watch such a show is it takes more than the desire to kill wildlife. It takes skill and brains and heart. That, to me, is where the show failed."

"You know we're asking for equal time to answer the documentary," Remington said. "We're going to state our side of the case in no uncertain terms."

"I hope you've sold it to sponsors," I said.

"We will. There isn't a company in America that would refuse to advertise on a program giving the hunters' side of the story."

"I wish I had a large company. I'd buy time on the show," I said.

"You know something," Remington said, "I think the Commies are behind the whole thing."

"But Tito hunts," I said.

"Sure, the Commie big shots hunt, but they would love to see hunting stopped in the United States. If they could turn Americans against hunting game, it would be the first step in a Red takeover of the United States."

"I guess you're right," I told Remington. "In a few years there wouldn't be a marksman left in America, and we'd all be left naked."

Remington looked at me suspiciously. "I thought you were against hunting."

"I am not," I replied. "As long as something gives people pleasure and you don't hurt anything, I say shoot."

COME AND GET ME, COPPER

As each day passes by, the automobile dealers are getting more desperate to move their cars. They've tried almost everything under the sun to no avail—well, almost everything.

"Attention, all cars—attention, all cars—go to Overview Terrace—a family is being held as hostage by a madman."

"Zipkind, we know you're in there. Throw your weapon out the window, and come out with your hands up, and you won't get hurt."

"Not unless the Friedkins agree to my terms."

"What are your terms?"

"They buy a new four-door Buccaneer station wagon with genuine leather seats, power steering, air conditioning, and white-wall tires. I'll throw in the radial tires for free."

"Zipkind, that is no way to sell an automobile."

"I've tried everything else, copper. I begged them to come into the showroom. I promised the greatest trade-in of their lives. I offered them financing over forty-eight months. But they just laughed at me. Well, now it's my turn to laugh. They either sign a contract or else. . . ."

"Listen to us, Zipkind. We'll talk about it later. Just let

the hostages go. We'll find you somebody else who might want to buy a station wagon."

"Don't kid me. Nobody wants to buy a station wagon now. The only thing the consumer understands is force. No one leaves this house unless I have a signed contract in my hand."

"Let me speak to Friedkin."

"Here he is, copper, but I warn you, if he makes one false move. . . ."

"Friedkin, are you willing to give in to Zipkind's demands?"

"I'd like to, Commissioner, but I don't have the money. Who can afford a new car these days?"

"He's stalling, copper. He's got the money; he just won't part with it. All right, if he can't afford a station wagon, what about a four-door Whiplash with vinyl bucket seats, disk brakes, and a rear-window defroster?"

"Zipkind, we can't negotiate with you for a new car until you release the hostages."

"Fie on you, copper. I'm going to move those cars off the lot one way or another."

"Zipkind, here is your wife, Esmerelda."

"Horace, please come out of the house. Even if you sell the Friedkins a car, you can't keep holding people as hostages every time you want to make a sale."

"No dice, Esmerelda. If I don't sell any cars, they'll take my dealership away from me. I have to think of us. I warned Friedkin something like this would happen if he kept stalling on the new models."

"Zipkind, we're losing patience with you. You either come out or we're coming in after you."

"All right, copper, I'm coming out. But Friedkin is going to be sorry. When he goes to buy his next new car, he'll be paying five hundred dollars more than they're selling for right now."

"Get in the cruiser, Zipkind. We're taking you down to headquarters."

"Hey, copper. What are you doing with a 1973 cruiser? How about a new Amazon? I'll throw in a siren and a red light gratis, and you get a two-year warranty on all parts except the engine. I'll give you eight hundred dollars for this heap, no questions asked."

"Sorry, Zipkind, but there's a freeze on in the department, and we can't buy any new cruisers."

"That's what I thought, copper. When it comes to a new car, you're all talk."

DOG DAYS IN LONDON

LONDON—London is now working on a problem that New York City has yet to seriously deal with. And that is what to do about dogs that do things on the sidewalk. This great metropolis has street inspectors who walk around their respective boroughs citing people whose dogs "have fouled the footpaths."

One of the greatest of all London's street inspectors is Mr. William James Parr of the borough of Camden. I saw Mr. Parr on television one night making his rounds and asked if I could accompany him for a few hours the next day. He kindly consented, and we met in front of the Camden town tube station.

Mr. Parr is a middle-aged modest man who neither glorifies his work nor puts down his job. If he can make London a cleaner place for people to walk, he feels he is earning the taxpayers' money.

The law is specific. "No one in charge of a dog shall allow it to foul the footpath."

Mr. Parr pounds the pavements every day, and when he spots a person and a suspicious dog, he follows them at a respectful distance. Only when the crime is actually committed will Mr. Parr approach the person and identify himself as a street inspector. "I wish to inform you of what I have seen." He'll point to the evidence and then will recount the details of the incident. Finally he will say, "Do you wish to challenge that?"

Whatever the person says Mr. Parr writes down in a book and promises that the statement shall appear in the report.

"You don't warn them of their constitutional rights?" I asked.

"No, I don't. It's not necessary when one deals with dog fouling."

"Suppose the person denies the dog belongs to him?"

"That's where observation is terribly important. If the dog is not on a leash but obeys the person's commands, it's obvious it belongs to the person charged. I then ask if there are any mitigating circumstances the person would like to lead."

"Such as?"

"Perhaps the dog has been constipated and fed a physic or a conditioning powder and can't control himself. I tell them all these facts will be reported to the town clerk."

"If it's a mad dog, can they plead insanity?" I asked.

"No," Mr. Parr replied.

"Would you spare a friend or a politician whose dog you caught in the act?"

Mr. Parr seemed shocked I would even suggest it.

"Certainly not. That wouldn't be fair. I do my job without favor or ill will."

"What reaction do you get from a person who has been cited?"

"Most people say, 'Oh, I'm terribly sorry.' A few might protest the dog was walking behind him and he hadn't noticed it, and once in a while they'll say, 'Why aren't you ever here when Stover's dog fouls?' "

"A dog lover would turn in his neighbor?" It was my turn to be shocked.

"I'm afraid so."

One of Mr. Parr's biggest problems is that he is the only one in the borough authorized to catch dogs fouling the walks.

"Most of the offenses," he told me, "take place at seven thirty to eight thirty in the morning and then in the evening at sunset. I work from eight thirty to four thirty, so I have to get up early on my own time if I want to catch many dogs in the act. Or stay late in the evening."

"When you follow a person and a dog, how can you be sure the dog will break the law?" I asked him.

"You have to have a sixth sense about these things," Mr. Parr replied.

When a person is cited, the town clerk then decides whether to bring it to trial. Most people, Mr. Parr said, plead guilty and throw their dogs on the mercy of the court. The fine could be as much as $40; but the person, unless he has a compulsive dog fouler, is never fined more than $5 or $10.

Camden is considered a high-dog-density area, and yet Mr. Parr has never lost a case.

He also has never been bitten by a dog or an owner. It is typical of England that despite the dangers of his profession, Mr. Parr does not carry a gun. Yet he performs one of the greatest services known to mankind. If New York City only had ten tall men like him.

DEAR VIRGINIA

It is only fitting at Christmastime that we discuss the famous "Dear Virginia" letter in which she asked a New York *Sun* editor whether or not there was a Santa Claus. Suppose Virginia would have written that letter today. Here are some of the possible replies:

From a U.S. Senator:

DEAR VIRGINIA:

Thank you so much for your letter of the 14th. I am always happy to hear from my constituents on the issues of the day. As you know, my feelings on Santa Claus have always been a matter of public record, and I intend to speak out on the subject at the appropriate time. But because we plan to hold hearings on this question, I believe it would be premature for me to tell you whether there is or is not a Santa Claus until we have all the facts. I am enclosing a speech I made on the floor of the Senate concerning new guidelines for alternate snow removal from our national highways. I thought you would be interested in this burning issue which affects all the citizens of our great state.

Sincerely yours

From the FBI:

DEAR VIRGINIA:

I regret to inform you that due to Federal Bureau of Investigation regulations we are not at liberty to disclose the information that you asked for. You may appeal this decision under the Freedom of Information Act if you so desire. In the meantime we are starting a file on you in which your letter is now listed as item No. 1. We are also opening a file on Santa Claus.

CLARENCE KELLEY

From the National Organization for Women:

DEAR VIRGINIA:

Your letter indicates your naïveté and lack of awareness of what has been going on in this country for the last 200 years. Santa Claus is an invention of the male supremist cabal to keep women from gaining full equality and respect. Only by rejecting the Santa Claus myth will we be able to overthrow the chains of bondage and free ourselves from the idea that it is the male who provides all the toys and other gifts on Christmas Eve. We invite you to attend the next meeting of NOW in your local community and learn the true facts of how we women bought the Santa Claus fairy tale and the price we are paying for it even today.

Sincerely yours

From the Department of Health, Education and Welfare:

DEAR VIRGINIA:

We regret we are unable to process your request for an answer to your question until you have filled out Form B1897 and Impact Application R9004567 as well as submitting Certification 459K as outlined in Paragraph 6, Page 198, Section 11 of Volume Four HEW Regulations. Once you have fulfilled these requirements your question shall be forwarded to the appropriate department.

But because of the pressure of work we advise you not to contact us again for eight months at the minimum. When you do, please refer to Serial 145923, which is the number your letter has been assigned.

Respectfully yours

From the *Encyclopaedia Britannica:*

DEAR VIRGINIA:

Thank you so much for your letter and the question you raised. The answer to it can be found in our new 26-volume edition which is now being offered at a special discount price. Not only will you find the answer to whether there is or is not a Santa Claus but you will find the answer to thousands of other questions that come up in everyday schoolwork and conversation. Our representative will be calling on you after the first of the year to advise you on our easy-term payment plan. This is one investment you'll never regret.

Sincerely

From the Post Office:

DEAR VIRGINIA:
We were unable to deliver your letter to the New York *Sun* as there was 5 cents postage due. Kindly weigh all letters in the future as rising costs make it impossible for us to deliver letters that are not properly stamped, especially on Saturday.

THE POSTMASTER GENERAL

GUN STAMPS FOR THE POOR

Jonathan Spear and Michael Petit have brought to my attention a statement from Harlon B. Carter of the National Rifle Association in defense of the "Saturday night special" handgun.

Carter told a House judiciary subcommittee on crime, "It makes no sense to me why possession of a finely made two-hundred-dollar handgun owned by a decent law-abiding man of means should be legal, but ownership of a forty-dollar handgun (Saturday night special) by an equally law-abiding resident of the inner city, who can't afford anything better to protect his family and home, should be a felony."

It is a very interesting point, and Spear and Petit have a solution to the problem.

The federal government should institute immediately a gun stamp program for the poor. The program would work as follows: A family of four making less than $6,000 a year would apply for gun stamps at the local post office.

All the head of the family would have to produce is his income tax return, and if he qualifies as a "needy case," he would be given the equivalent of $200 in gun stamps, which he could spend at any gun store for weapons and ammunition. The gun store would be reimbursed by the government for the stamps at 100 cents on the dollar.

Some people might argue that the poor would take advantage of the program and use the stamps to buy cheap guns and pocket the rest of the money. But while there may be some abuses of the gun stamp program, it would still be the best and cheapest way of seeing that no American citizen, no matter what his financial status, would be deprived of his right to bear arms.

It is hard to believe that in a country as rich as ours there are perhaps as many as 50,000,000 people who go to bed every night without a gun under their pillows. Many of the poor are to blame for this condition. They would rather buy food with their money than guns. But a majority are not responsible for their plight. Many are jobless, elderly, and children. They have tried to acquire guns, but the cost, even for a Saturday night special, has been beyond their means.

In the past the middle class has ignored them in the belief that anyone who really wants a gun should pull himself up by his bootstraps and earn one. But in an urban society during a period of cruel inflation it's not as easy to acquire a decent gun as it used to be. We can no longer stand idly by and say to these poor people, "You can't have a gun unless you buy it yourself, the way we did."

Gun stamps are the obvious solution to helping people who can't help themselves. At first it would be considered demeaning to some to accept gun handouts from the government. But as time went on, I believe that poor people would accept gun stamps in the same way they accept food stamps—as a temporary way of providing their families with the basic necessities of life. They would no longer feel themselves inferior to the decent law-abiding man of means who can afford a $200 weapon. They will have the opportunity, which they have been deprived of so long, of using their guns to settle family arguments without resorting to knives and hammers.

Gun stamps will bring dignity and joy to their lives.

The next question is cost. Can the United States afford a gun stamp program? The answer is yes. For one thing it will be a big boost to the handgun industry in this country, providing hundreds of thousands of jobs for people. It will also encourage new ammunition factories to be built in depressed areas. A subsidized gun program in this country will give manufacturers an incentive to speed up production and will guarantee them a profit in lean years when weapon sales are down.

So not only the poor but everybody will benefit from gun stamps.

No country can boast it has done all for its people until it arms every man, woman, and child with a weapon. So if you really care for the plight of the poor, as Harlon B. Carter of the NRA does, write to your congressman today.

16

Celebrities in Washington

FLOGGING BOOKS

Sally is in California, Ben is in Rochester, Irwin is in Philadelphia, Saul is in Greensboro, Myra is in Pittsburgh, Jimmy is in Hartford, and Gail is in Baton Rouge.

What are all these people doing? They're flogging their books—that's what. There was a time when a person wrote a book and sold it to a publisher who printed and distributed it. The writer's work was finished the day he delivered the manuscript.

But since television, writing is just a small part of an author's business. His or her major effort must now go into the selling of the book, which means crisscrossing the United States for a month or six weeks, appearing on talk shows that start at seven in the morning and radio shows that go on at midnight.

This is how it goes. After your book is accepted for publication, the publisher takes your editor away from you and turns you over to the "TV and radio coordinator" in the publicity department, usually a man or woman who has just started there the week before. The reason for this is the biggest turnover in the book industry is in the publicity department. And the reason for this is that every time a book doesn't sell, the first people to be fired are the publicists.

The coordinator, who hasn't had time to read your book, tells you that he/she has arranged for you to be on *Bob Dimplehoffer's All Night FM Radio Talk Show* in Corn Blight, Nebraska. The coordinator tells you Dimplehoffer is very high on your book and specifically asked for you to be on the show.

You ask how to get to Corn Blight, Nebraska, and he/she tells you it's very easy. You fly to Chicago and change planes for Omaha. In Omaha you change planes for Lincoln. Then you take a Greyhound bus to Waring Falls and change to a Trailways bus to Sundown Corners, where one of Bob's people will pick you up and drive you the ninety miles to Corn Blight.

If you raise any objections, the coordinator says, "Well, if you don't want to sell any books, that's your business."

So you kiss your wife and children good-bye and promise them you'll be home by Christmas.

After missing the connection in Chicago and the Greyhound bus in Lincoln, you finally make it to Dimplehoffer's radio station in Corn Blight with a half hour to spare. Dimplehoffer is in the studio playing a Bobby Gentry record. He says, "Look, I only got a couple minutes, fill me in on what the book is all about."

"Didn't you read it?"

"Are you kidding? I don't have time to read the papers. It's about Watergate, isn't it?"

"No, that was my last book. This one is about a cat who does TV commercials and gets kidnapped."

"But I thought I was going to talk to you about Watergate. My listeners don't want to hear about cats— not at three in the morning."

"But the cat book is the one I want to flog."

"All right, but make it short. I have to take telephone calls about Mrs. Ford's attitudes toward young people."

After Bobby Gentry, Dimplehoffer says, "We have a special guest who's just written a book about dogs."

"Cats."

"Right, cats. What brings you to Corn Blight, Art?"

"I was just passing through and I had never seen an FM radio station before. . . ."

The next morning after three hours' sleep you go into the local bookstore (the only bookstore) to autograph your book.

"What book?" the lady asks.

"Didn't my publisher tell you I was coming here to plug my book?"

"Nope. We only handle best-sellers."

Three days later you get back home and call the TV and radio coordinator. "They had no books in the stores," you scream.

He/she says calmly, "That's not my department. You have to speak to sales."

JUNK MAIL

Even important people get junk mail. Through the courtesy of the CIA I am able to provide some samples of mail that were thrown away before they were fully read:

HENRY KISSINGER

WASHINGTON, D.C.

DEAR MR. KISSINGER,

This is your golden opportunity. We are offering at a special discount *Power and How to Use It,* a most informative book for people who are lacking in self-confidence and are afraid to stand out in a crowd. Learn how to seize the initiative in dealing with other people. You no longer have to take a back seat to your friends and strangers. In six weeks you could become another. . . .

RICHARD NIXON

SAN CLEMENTE, CALIFORNIA

DEAR MR. NIXON

Have you ever thought how much simpler your life would be if you had a tape recorder? If you act now we will send you for ten days, free of charge, one of our Simplex Recorders, which you can use not only to dictate letters into but also to record conversations with friends and associates. By pressing a button the machine activates itself and. . . .

ABE BEAME

NEW YORK CITY

DEAR MR. BEAME,

Gerald Ford and the Republican Party need your help. Your contribution, whether $5 or $100, will assure the election for the next four years of a man who. . . .

NELSON ROCKEFELLER

WASHINGTON, D.C.

DEAR MR. ROCKEFELLER,

Our new shipment of beds has just arrived and we know you'll be interested. Thanks to a Pre-Thanksgiving Day warehouse sale you can now purchase a unique bed that is not only for sleeping but is a work of art. The mattress is actually a mirror, and the canopy above it has see-through glass so you can look at the ceiling while resting on your stomach. There are six oars attached to the sides of the bed and a lifeboat hanging over the headboard. At the foot of the bed is a curved movie screen attached to a shower nozzle. It comes in king size, queen size and. . . .

Ralph Nader

Washington, D.C.

Dear Mr. Nader,

Have you ever thought about buying a Harley-Davidson 30 XL motorcycle? You're only as young as you feel, and once you roar off on one of our 1976 models, you will know the thrill of. . . .

The Maharishi Yogi

c/o Post Office

New Delhi

Are you feeling tense, nervous and unable to cope with life? Why not take up golf? We have a few memberships still open at the Rolling Hills Country Club. . . .

Fidel Castro

Havana, Cuba

Dear Mr. Castro,

It's never too early to think about life insurance. Perhaps you're one of those people who keep saying, "Nothing can happen to me." But in these times of uncertainty why not assure yourself of protection while it's still available? Just send back this postcard and one of our agents will be happy to call on you and. . . .

Patty Hearst

San Francisco, California.

Dear Patty,

Are you the girl your parents think you are? If not, a subscription to *Seventeen* magazine might be your answer. We tell you the secrets of growing up and how to make your teen years the most exciting of your life. We also tell you. . . .

THE SECRET DOVE

If Nelson Rockefeller keeps it up, he could become our greatest Vice President since Spiro Agnew. Just the other day he explained to the National Urban Coalition that the reason he did not criticize American involvement in Vietnam in the 1960s was that he feared he would harm New York State's chances of obtaining federal aid.

"I was elected governor of New York, and my responsibility was to the people of New York," he was quoted as saying. "You don't kick people in Washington in the shins if you expect them to do something for you." He added, "I think I did a pretty good job if I do say so myself." Rockefeller claimed that during his administration the state increased its aid from the federal government from 5 cents on each dollar of taxes paid by the state to eighteen cents.

When the questioner told the Vice President he was disappointed that Rockefeller failed to speak out while the government was spending $150 billion and 50,000 lives on the war in Vietnam, the Vice President shot back, "I can see you never ran for political office, young man."

One's sympathies can go out to Rockefeller, who as governor of New York had to keep quiet on the war to get his state as much money as he could. There must have been some terrible soul-searching during those difficult years of the sixties.

"Governor, the students are up in arms about the war; there are demonstrations in every city, and we just keep pouring in more men to no avail. Don't you think you ought to come out with a statement against U.S. involvement in Vietnam?"

"Oh, God, I wish I could. But I have to think of the state first. We need some more money for our highways, and I'm not going to kick those guys in Washington in the shins right now."

"Couldn't you say it in such a way that they wouldn't get angry?"

"I've thought and thought about it, but you don't know how sensitive the White House is. One word from me about the war and we'll lose the Brooklyn Navy Yard. I've got a good relationship with President Johnson, and he just gave me five more veterans' hospitals. I'm not about to blow it with some stupid statement that could only get him sore at me. That war means a lot to Johnson, and he's been pretty good to anyone who supports him. But one peep out of me, and we could lose one hundred million dollars in urban renewal."

"You're a good governor, sir. The easy thing would be to speak out against the war. The tough thing is to remain quiet and get all the federal money you can."

"Someday those same students who are demonstrating in the streets are going to say, 'Thank the Lord Rocky kept his mouth shut about the war. Otherwise, we never would have had a new post office in Albany!' "

"The war won't go on forever, Governor, but you've given New York monuments for the future."

"Why don't those kids understand when you run for political office you have to please those who are in charge of the purse strings? I could say the war is a waste of money and lives. I could say we ought to get out of there right away. But if I did, where would we get the money to fix up Jones Beach?"

"They'd cut you off without a dime, Governor. If the world only knew you were a secret dove."

"Someday I'll be able to tell them how I really felt about the war. Someday they'll realize that I knew in my heart it was wrong and stupid and immoral. But I can't do it now—not while the Long Island Railroad is in trouble."

"Sir, President Johnson is on the phone."

"Mr. President, Rocky here. You people really did a great job on that Tet offensive. I couldn't have been more thrilled. . . . You'll have that coonskin on the wall before you know it. . . . What? You want to give me a new dam for Niagara Falls. Aw, Mr. President, you shouldn't."

JACKIE AS EDITOR

I have a book publisher friend of mine in New York named Binding who was very upset that Viking had hired Jackie Kennedy Onassis as an editor.

"If I had known she was available for two hundred dollars a week," he said, "I would have hired her. I thought she would ask for two hundred and fifty dollars."

"Even if Jackie asked for two hundred and fifty dollars," I said, "it still would have been a bargain."

"I'm not so sure," said Binding. "Suppose she decides to decorate her own office. You can't give Jackie Onassis a steel desk and a swivel chair. You'd have to find a Louis the Fifteenth desk that came out of Versailles and a chair to match. Then you would have to have a sofa from Marie Antoinette's bedroom and at least one Pissarro and one Cézanne for the walls."

"Don't forget the drapes and carpeting," I said.

"I'm afraid the Viking office manager is going to have to go to Parke-Bernet auction sales for the next six months," Binding told me.

"It's still worth it," I said. "Jackie has to be an asset to the firm. Everyone will send her their new manuscripts."

"Why?"

"Do you realize what a rejection slip from Jackie Onassis would be worth to Charles Hamilton Autographs Unlimited?"

"I never thought of that," Binding said, "but still Viking is going to have problems. Jackie really doesn't think like a publisher. I can see an agent calling up and demanding ten thousand dollars for a first book and Jackie saying, 'We'll give you fifty thousand dollars.' "

"It could happen," I agreed.

"She also doesn't know how writers operate. You have to be on their backs all the time, and many authors won't even take any calls from their editors because they don't have any pages to send them. I think it's going to be a terrible blow to Jackie when she telephones her writer and he tells his wife to tell Jackie he isn't there. She's not used to people refusing her calls."

"It will be tough at first," I admitted, "but she's going to have to take rejection like everybody else in the business."

"Then," said Binding, "let's not forget the lunches. Most editors do their business over lunch, and they're expected to pick up the tab. Jackie is not going to take writers to Schraffts."

"I'd love to be Jackie's writer," I said, "just so I could go to Twenty-one for lunch every day. What kind of books do you think Viking will ask Jackie to find for them?"

"I heard her first project was going to be a travel book called *Europe on $15,000 a Day,*" Binding said.

"It could sell," I said.

"I think another thing Jackie is going to have to face up to is that writers are very sensitive, unhappy people and they take out most of their frustrations on their editors. If the publisher doesn't advertise a book, the writers scream like mad."

"You mean people are going to scream at Jackie?"

"You better believe it. I've never known a writer who didn't scream at his or her editor."

"But nobody screams at Jackie!" I said.

"They will now. And don't forget about writer's block. Every writer gets a block sooner or later, and then his editor has to go see him and unblock him."

"I wonder if Jackie knows how to unblock a writer."

"She's going to have to learn," Binding said.

"You know, Binding, I think you're just jealous because Jackie didn't go with your firm."

"I suppose you're right. I think what I'll do is let her break in at Viking, and then when she gets the hang of it, I'll offer her three hundred dollars a week. It's a lot of money, but in the book business everything's a gamble."

CELEBRITIES IN WASHINGTON

Something is happening in Washington. For the first time newspapermen are becoming more famous than the people they write about. I don't know if you can credit Spiro Agnew or the Nixon White House gang for the trend, but it's having a tremendous effect on the business, and some journalists are finding it difficult to handle their celebrity status.

As soon as Burt Brillo broke the story on the break-in of the Wesley Heights Taco Hut, he was besieged by other reporters wanting to do profiles on him. Brillo, who happened to be a police reporter at the time, achieved stardom overnight by discovering that the Taco Hut had been used by the CIA to feed their midnight-to-8 A.M. shift. While this in itself would have been enough to make it a front-page story, a source whom Brillo has yet to name leaked the fact that two of the employees of the Taco Hut had entered the United States illegally from Mexico.

It was luck plus perseverance that made Brillo the most talked about man in Washington.

Besides getting a book contract to write the story of how he broke the story, Brillo was also signed up for a lecture tour and was interviewed by Barbara Walters, Mike Douglas, Dinah Shore, Merv Griffin, and Johnny Carson—all on the same day.

Through his press agent I managed to get an interview with Burt in his ranch house overlooking Capitol Hill.

The press agent warned me I could only spend thirty minutes with him as *Women's Wear Daily* was going to take pictures at five o'clock.

I didn't know what to expect when I rang the doorbell, but I was pleasantly surprised to find Brillo a warm, sensitive human being who hadn't allowed all the adulation to go to his head.

We sat by the swimming pool, and a Japanese man-servant brought us gin and tonics.

"Most people," he said, "think that newspapermen are different. But actually I'm just like anyone else except I live better and pay more taxes. Sure, I was lucky in the Taco Hut break-in, but I find in this business you're only as good as your next story. That's why I'm being very careful what I choose for my next assignment. Oh, I've been offered lots of reporting jobs, but they're all junk— bank robberies, embezzlements, espionage trials, and even a war or two. But I'm not about to rush into anything. I have to think of my future."

"Mr. Brillo, there was a rumor that Omar Sharif was going to play you in the movies. How do you feel about that?"

"Omar tried to buy the story, but I don't think he'd be right for it. I told the producers if they could get Al Pacino or Steve McQueen, I would be interested. I don't want to make the error Woodward and Bernstein did by having two nobodies like Robert Redford and Dustin Hoffman portray them. Most police reporters make the mistake of selling their stories without casting approval."

"What's the toughest thing about being a successful newspaperman?" I asked.

"The lack of privacy. I can't go out to the store without being mobbed by my fans. Of course, they're the people who made me and I shouldn't complain, but sometimes I wish I was back to being just plain Burt Brillo again, covering the Third Police Precinct on the lobster shift."

"I guess you're bothered by a lot of female admirers, too."

"What investigative reporter isn't? But after a while the thrill wears off, and you wish you could find someone who would love you for yourself and not just because you're the author of the Taco Hut story."

A tall, leggy blonde came over to us. "Mr. Brillo, your barber is here."

I apologized for keeping him so long.

Brillo gave me a wide toothy smile and a warm handclasp.

"That's perfectly all right. I used to be a newspaperman myself."

A TIP FOR NIXON'S TRIP

Former President Richard Nixon is preparing for his trip to the People's Republic of China. I wonder if he will write any poems for Mao Tse-tung. Here are a few for Mr. Nixon in case he doesn't have the time.

Once again I stand at the Great Wall
Made from centuries of stone.
Confucius says, "Those who stonewall
Will receive a thousand pardons."

The Chinese greet me with open arms
And throw pink rose petals at my feet.
Why do all forsake me,
Save the Teamsters and the Red Guard?

If winter has come to cold Peking,
Can David Frost be far behind?
The wind blows across the Forbidden City.
The earth groans and twists while ice-laden.

Rivers rush down to meet the sea.
A cloud crosses the sky.
I wonder how much money Rabbi Korff has raised for
me in Toledo?

I sit in the Great Hall feasting on Peking duck.
How good it is compared to San Clemente crow.

I can testify to the beauty of China,
I can testify to the goodness of Mao,
I can testify to the greatness of Chou,
I can testify to the wisdom of Teng,
But I can't testify in Washington, D.C.,
Because my health forbids me to travel.

Why have I come back to this strange land
Shrouded in mystery and silence?
Cloaked in a thousand secrets
Of ten thousand years or more?
Because it beats the devil out of
Writing my book.

I have seen peasants work with their hoes,
I have seen steelworkers work with their backs,
I have seen dockworkers work with their shoulders,
I have seen women work with their men,
Yet I have not seen one person in all China
Ask me what was on the eighteen minutes of Rosemary's
   tape.

The hawk flies across the sky,
Waiting to swoop down and make its kill.
Trees sway in the wind and watch and wait
As tiny birds sing sad songs of yesterday.
So why won't the Supreme Court
Give me back my personal papers?

As night falls over the Yangtze
And a wolf cries out in Tibet,

The fires of the sun become embers,
And the embers become ashes.
And from the ashes a great man will rise again.
I'll bet you can't guess who it will be?

17

Party Stoppers

COLLECT CALL

"Hello, I have a collect call from Miss Joyce Robinson in Oshkosh, Wisconsin. Will you accept the charges?"

"Yes, operator, we will."

"Hi, Pops. How are you?"

"Fine. What are you doing in Oshkosh? I thought you were driving to Cape Cod to visit Aunt Rose."

"We were, but Cynthia wanted to stop off and visit a boy she knew from school who lives in Minneapolis."

"Who is Cynthia?"

"She's a girl I met in New Orleans."

"New Orleans? I didn't know you went to New Orleans."

"I wasn't planning to, but Tommy said there was a great concert of the Grateful Dead scheduled to play in the stadium. He got the day right, but the wrong month."

"Tommy?"

"He was hitchhiking on Ninety-five."

"You started out with Ellen Mulberry. Where is she?"

"She met some kids she knew in Fort Lauderdale, and they were driving to Mexico, so she decided to go with them."

"Do Mr. and Mrs. Mulberry know this?"

"I think Ellen called them after the accident."

"What accident?"

"The camper she was in had a blowout, and Ellen got banged up a little."

"So you're now traveling with Cynthia and Tommy."

"No. Tommy stayed in New Orleans, and Cynthia left yesterday. She said she couldn't wait until my car was fixed."

"What's wrong with your car?"

"The motor fell out. That's what I'm calling you about. The garageman said it will cost five hundred and fifty dollars to fix it up."

"That's a fortune!"

"You don't have to pay it if you don't want to. I can leave the car here. I met a guy who has a motorcycle, and he says he'll take me as far as Detroit."

"I'LL PAY IT!"

"How's Mom?"

"She's on the extension. I think she was fine until we got your call. Where are you staying until you get your car fixed?"

"I met some nice kids who have a religious commune near here, and they said I could stay with them if I promise to devote the rest of my life to God."

"That's nice."

"The only problem is I have to shave my head."

"Can't you stay at a motel?"

"I don't have any money left."

"What happened to the three hundred dollars I gave you?"

"Two hundred went for expenses, and one hundred of it went for the fine."

"What fine?"

"We were fined one hundred dollars for speeding in this little itty-bitty town in Arkansas."

"I told you not to drive fast."

"I wasn't driving. Fred was."

"Who the hell is Fred?"

"He's a vegetarian, and he says capitalism is finished in the West."

"That's worth one hundred dollars to hear. Are you going to Cape Cod to visit Aunt Rose or aren't you?"

"As soon as I get the car fixed, Pops. Send me the money care of Western Union. You don't want the man to fix the dented door at the same time?"

"Your car had no dented door."

"It does now. I have to go, Dad. Some kids I met are going to take me white-water canoeing. Good-bye. And, Pops—have a nice day."

DOG DAYS AT CHRISTMAS

It used to be that college students brought their friends home for the holidays. Now they bring home their dogs. The dogs are a little harder to deal with than the friends.

I thought I was the only parent who had the problem, but Fernwood, my neighbor, told me the dog problem is quite serious at his house, too.

"Felicia is coming home on Thursday," he told me.

"That's nice," I said.

"I'm not sure. She's bringing her Labrador, Shakespeare, with her. Shakespeare weighs two hundred pounds, and he makes my wife very nervous. He also isn't housebroken."

"That's terrible."

"It isn't Shakespeare's fault," Fernwood told me. "Felicia lives in a dormitory which does not require dogs to be housebroken. At least that's what she told us the last time she was home. She said that there were four other dogs living in the dorm, and none of them was trained to go outside."

"Why do you think that is?" I asked.

"I believe most colleges don't pay too much attention to what dogs do on campus."

"But you would think discovering how to housebreak a dog would be a much more valuable learning experience than the rise and fall of the Roman Empire."

"It is at my house, but it doesn't seem to be at the university. My daughter is far more concerned with what the aerosol companies are doing to the ozone than what Shakespeare does in our living room."

"I'm with you," I told Fernwood. "My daughter won't come home unless she can bring her dog, Hobo, with her. This presents many problems, the least of which is that we can't go anywhere during the holiday season where dogs are unwelcome. This limits us quite a bit. My niece was getting married, and when she said she didn't want any dogs at the wedding, my daughter got very angry and refused to go with us. She said although she could understand her cousin acting that way she could never explain it to Hobo."

Fernwood said, "My problem is my son, Carlton, is also coming home from school for Christmas, and he's bringing his dog, Neptune. Neptune is a white German shepherd and can't stand my daughter's dog, Shakespeare. My daughter thinks Carlton purposely turned Neptune against Shakespeare, and now there is bad feeling between the children."

"Is Neptune housebroken?" I asked.

"Carlton says he is, but when he sees what Shakespeare does, Neptune says, 'The hell with it.' "

"Why do you think all the college kids are into dogs?" I asked Fernwood.

"Beats me. I guess it's easier for them to relate to dogs than it is to people. When I went to college, we used to like girls. The only time you had a dog was when you were a little kid and weren't old enough to have a girl."

"That's the way it was with me," I said. "The minute I lost my interest in dogs, I knew I was ready to go out with girls."

"Today," said Fernwood, "the kids date much earlier,

and then, when they get bored with each other, they start going out with dogs."

"Maybe it's just a passing fad," I suggested. "Maybe in a year or two they'll bring home goldfish for Christmas instead."

"I hope you're right," Fernwood said, "because I'm not sure I can keep paying the rug cleaning bill for school vacations."

DINNER IN PARIS

PARIS—The last time I was in Paris, six years ago, I wrote a column titled "Paris on $500 a Day." The thrust of the piece was that it was still possible to get by in the French capital on $500 if you passed up lunch. My French friends, as well as Americans living in France, thought the article was very funny. But they aren't laughing anymore.

When it comes to inflation, the United States is *Mary Poppins* and France is *Deep Throat*.

But if you don't worry about prices, you can still have a marvelous time in Paris. What you have to do is forget everything and just decide to live for the moment.

I did this the first night I arrived in town. My wife and I went to a small bistro that boasted two stars in the *Guide Michelin*.

When the waiter gave us the menu, I thought he made a mistake.

"I beg your pardon, monsieur," I said. "But I believe you have made an error. You gave me the Bank of France's financial report for the month of May."

"No, monsieur, that is the *carte pour* dinner."

My wife, who always gets nervous when she sees melon selling for more than $15 a portion, whispered to me, "Let's get out of here."

"Don't be silly. We don't get to Paris very often. Let's

enjoy it." I studied the menu carefully. "Now we have our choice. We can have the white asparagus or send Joel to college in the fall."

She said, "You mean to say that white asparagus costs as much as Joel's tuition?"

"Yes," I replied, "but they're the large white ones with Hollandaise sauce. You can only get them in the spring."

"But," my wife, always the practical one, said, "Joel had his heart set on going to college."

"Look, Joel can go to school anytime. But how often do we come to France and have a chance to order white asparagus? I know if we explain it to him, he'll understand."

There were so many dishes to choose from after the first course that I couldn't make up my mind.

Finally, I said to my wife, "Remember that house we were going to buy in Martha's Vineyard?"

"The one overlooking the ocean?"

"That's the one." I said. "Let's have the lobster instead."

"You mean you'd rather have lobster than own a house on Martha's Vineyard?"

"But this lobster is cooked in a special cream sauce of the chef. It could be years before we have a lobster like this again. We have to think of our old age."

"I don't know," my wife said. "I had my heart set on that house."

"Well, I have my heart set on lobster, and since they're both the same price, I think our stomachs should come first."

The waiter handed me the wine card.

"There's a very nice Pouilly-Fuissé," I said.

"Can we afford it?" my wife asked.

"We can if we sell the car when we get back home."

"I need a car," she protested.

"All right," I said. "We'll order an inexpensive Sancerre and cancel the orthodontist's work on Connie's teeth."

My wife was becoming agitated. "If it's costing this much for dinner, how are we going to pay our hotel bill?"

"Will you stop worrying? What do you think the World Bank is for?"

TWENTY YEARS LATER

PARIS—One of the main reasons I went back to Paris in 1974 was to celebrate the twentieth anniversary of the breaking of the six-minute Louvre. It was exactly twenty years ago to the day that a young American student named Peter Stone amazed the world by going through the Louvre museum in five minutes and nineteen seconds.

As everyone knows, there are only three things worth seeing in the Louvre museum—the "Venus de Milo," the "Winged Victory," and the "Mona Lisa." The rest of the stuff is all junk.

For years tourists have been trying to get through the Louvre as quickly as possible, see those three things, and then go out shopping again.

Before World War II the record for going through the Louvre was seven minutes and fourteen seconds. But after the war, as clothes got lighter and cameras got smaller, people kept cutting down the time, and in 1948 a man known as the Swedish Cannonball, paced by his Welsh wife, did it in six minutes and twelve seconds. For the first time there was serious talk of breaking the six-minute Louvre.

But it was to be four more years. On June 18, 1954, Peter Stone, under perfect tourist conditions, literally flew through the Louvre, around the "Venus de Milo," up past the "Winged Victory," down to the "Mona Lisa," and back out again into a waiting taxi. He achieved the impossible, bringing fame and wealth to himself and glory to his country.

President Eisenhower personally sent him a telegram which read: "I rejoice with all Americans at your amazing feat. You're what the United States is all about."

So here I was twenty years later at the Louvre museum with Peter Stone to relive that great moment in history.

Stone, now middle-aged, paunchy, and slightly gray, went unrecognized by most of the tourists who were going through the Louvre. As we went over the same course, he noted, "It's all different now. There are very few American tourists anymore, and it's only a matter of time before the Japanese will take the record away from us."

"Peter, I was there the day you broke the six-minute Louvre," I said. "I remember your telling me at the time that you were going to do it. What made you so sure?"

"I had discovered something that nobody else knew," he said as we walked around the "Venus de Milo," "and that was you didn't have to pay admission on Sunday mornings to get into the Louvre. In that way I could cut twenty seconds from my time. The second thing I did was leave the film out of my camera. I carried less weight than other tourists. Finally, I had developed a nonskid sneaker in the States so I could make the sharp turns around the 'Winged Victory' without slipping on the marble."

We walked up the marble staircase past the "Winged Victory." "This is where I made up thirty seconds," Peter said. "Most tourists look at the back of the 'Winged Victory,' but I said to myself, 'If you've seen one "Winged Victory," you've seen them all,' and I just whizzed by without stopping."

"What did you do after you broke the six-minute Louvre?" I asked Peter.

"I did some exhibition running at the Prado in Spain and the Tate Gallery in London. The Russians invited me to run through the Hermitage in Leningrad. It was the first time the Soviets had ever asked an American to race through one of their museums. But it was during the height of the cold war, and John Foster Dulles wouldn't let me do it."

"So here it is twenty years later. What happens to a Louvre champ as time goes on?"

Peter replied, "The legs go first, then the wind, and finally the eyes. I doubt if I can get through the Louvre in ten minutes now in any condition."

We arrived at where the "Mona Lisa" hung when Peter had broken the record. The picture wasn't there! I asked an old guard, "Where is the 'Mona Lisa'?"

The guard shrugged his shoulders and replied, "In Japan."

Tears came to Peter's eyes as he said, "It figures."

PARTY STOPPERS

It's very hard at a party to get any attention. Nothing shocks people anymore, and you really have to be on your toes to get somebody to listen to you.

I realized this the other night when I was at dinner and someone turned to Don Cook and said, "Where are you going after you leave Washington?"

"Los Angeles," he replied. This landed like a dull thud until he added, "By train."

Everybody dropped his knife and fork, and suddenly Cook was the man of the hour.

It got me to thinking about party stoppers, things you can say which will make people sit up and take notice. Here are a few for starters.

"I still think Nixon is innocent."

"The electric company just notified me that it was lowering my rates."

"Nelson Rockefeller has asked me to write a book."

"I sold Wilbur Mills my car."

"If Henry Kissinger calls, tell him I'm not here."

"I played softball with Robert Vesco last week."

"Earl Butz told me a funny story the other day."

"I get forty-five miles to the gallon."

"Arnold Palmer borrowed my putter."

"Billie Jean King always has trouble with my second serve."

"I just hired Spiro Agnew to work for me."

"General Brown spoke at our synagogue last night."

"My son has never smoked pot."

"My husband has never looked at another woman."

"Woodward and Bernstein dropped by the house the other morning to ask me some questions."

"I talked to a man who read J. Edgar Hoover's diary."

"I'm going to have a vasectomy."

"I shared a taxi the other day with Howard Hughes."

"I gave Jerry Ford a piece of chewing gum once, when he was House minority leader."

"Bobby Fischer hates my opening move."

"My daughter works in a massage parlor."

"The shah of Iran owes me ten dollars."

"Gloria Steinem irons my shirts."

"I went duck hunting with Lieutenant Calley last weekend."

"My brother drives a school bus in Boston."

"Masters and Johnson asked me to volunteer for an interesting experiment."

"Ann Landers just called me up, and she was crying."

"The CIA rented my house."

"John Dean used to be my lawyer."

"My cousin is Linda Lovelace's dentist."

"I flew in from Chicago with Erica Jong."

"Billy Graham is in my Bible class."

"My sister and her fiancé are going to be married by Judge Sirica."

"Jane Fonda joined our American Legion Women's Auxiliary."

"The Secret Service wants a list of my guests in advance."

"Ronald Reagan gave me a subscription to *Rolling Stone.*"

"Patty Hearst is getting awfully fat."

THE WAR OF THE STONES

I had a kidney stone attack in Evansville, Indiana. I wouldn't have even mentioned it except that an alert Associated Press urology correspondent picked up the story, and it made the AP wire. So many people have written in asking what a kidney stone attack really feels like that I decided to try to explain it in terms that the layman can understand.

A kidney stone is about the size of a tiny pebble to everyone except the person who has one. To this person it is the size of the Rock of Gibraltar. In fact, many people when they get a kidney stone attack scream out, "I've got a piece of the Rock."

There are two kinds of kidney stones. One is made up of uric acid, and the other of calcium. Doctors can differentiate between the two, but patients can't, nor at the time of an attack do they give a damn. If you've felt one kidney stone, you've felt them all.

This is what seems to happen as far as the victim is concerned. He is going along minding his own business when suddenly, out of nowhere, a mountain forms in the kidney which, as I said, feels like the size of the Rock of Gibraltar.

The kidney reacts angrily to this interference with its function and tries to push the rock into what might be described as the Suez Canal. Obviously the Suez Canal cannot accommodate the Rock of Gibraltar, and without any warning war is declared between the kidney and the rock.

An urgent message is sent on the hot line from the kidney to the rock. "Unless you get out of our canal immediately, we will attack with everything we have in our organ."

The rock sends back a one-word reply: "NUTS!"

The patient, who is a horrified neutral spectator to this exchange, tries everything to achieve peace. He paces up and down, rolls to and fro, and eventually tries to climb the wall in hopes that the kidney and rock will come to their senses.

Using Kissinger diplomatic tactics, the patient tries to persuade the rock that if it will just move a few inches down the canal, the kidney will not try to break it up.

But the rock is adamant and demands tremendous concessions in exchange for withdrawing from its position.

"How do I know," the rock asks, "that if I move from where I am now I will not be driven into the sea?"

The victim assures the rock the kidney has no intention of pushing it into the sea. All the kidney wants to do is live in peace with the lower part of the body. As long as the rock doesn't try to prevent the kidney from doing its work, the rock can live in the bladder for as long as it wants to.

If negotiations fail and the rock refuses to move, then a UN doctor is called in who immediately fires a volley of Demerol or some other painkiller into the bloodstream.

This does not stop the war between the rock and the kidney, but it gives some shelter to the innocent, while the kidney tries to push the enemy out of its territory. This can only be done with gallons of water which the kidney forces against the rock.

If the good guy (the kidney) wins, the rock will retreat and even sue for peace. If the rock is able to repulse the water attack and hold its own, then the kidney will have to surrender, which means handing over negotiations to the Blue Cross.

It would be nice to report that once a kidney stone has

lost a battle others would learn their lesson. But unfortunately this is not the case. Even though my kidney moved the enemy to a safe place, I distinctly heard in my Demerol stupor the rock say to the kidney, "I may go down the drain, but there's a lot more of us where I came from."

THE SUMMER OF '76

"Hey, Marge, Patrick's home from college."

"Patrick, Patrick, my, you've grown a beard. It looks very, very, very grown-up, doesn't it, George?"

"Yes, it does. It makes you look like a real man. Here, Patrick, let me help you with your bags."

"Patrick, I put new draperies on your windows, and I bought a new rug for your floor. And I cooked a big roast beef for you.

"Why don't you take a nice bath and we'll all have dinner and you can tell us all about school?"

"It's good to have you home, son. The house has been a morgue without you. I had the pool table recovered; maybe we can have a few games this week?"

"He's tired, George. Let him go upstairs and get cleaned up. You seem so thin, Patrick. We're going to have to fatten you up."

"How are you fixed for cash, son? Here's twenty bucks. You probably want to go out and have a few beers with your pals."

"Maybe he'd like to have a party, George. He could invite over all his friends from high school."

"Sure thing, Marge, and we could play some tennis. I think I can still beat you, son."

"Go upstairs, Patrick, and make yourself at home. My, it's good to see him, isn't it, George?"

"You can say that again, Marge."

(One week later)

"Hello, George. Was it sweltering at the office?"

"Yup. Where's Patrick?"

"He's up in his room sleeping."

"At six o'clock in the evening?"

"I think he got in around four this morning."

"He gets in at four every morning. What are we running around here, a Playboy Club for teenagers?"

"Now, George, don't get angry again. He had a very rough semester, and he's just trying to relax."

"I had a rough semester, too, but I don't stay out until four in the morning. Did you talk to him about the empty wine bottles in the car?"

"He said only two belonged to him. I must say he looks worse now than when he came home from school."

"And what about a job? Did you ask him if he was looking for a job?"

"He said he's been looking, George."

"I'll bet. You know there are very few employment offices open at eight o'clock at night."

"Well, he says he's been trying very hard, but no one wants to hire him."

"Why should they with that damn beard? If he shaved it off and looked presentable, maybe he could find something."

"Hush, he might hear you!"

"I couldn't care less if he heard me or not. He needs someone to kick his rear in. I worked in the summer when I went to college."

(Two weeks later)

"Have you seen Patrick today, Marge?"

"No, but I saw him in the kitchen yesterday with his pals. They ate everything in the icebox."

"It figures. When does he go back to school?"

"Not until September."

"Good grief. You mean he's going to be here two *more* months?"

"It seems like a long time, George, but July and August will go very fast."

"I'm not too certain. It seems when they're away, time just whistles by. But when they're home, it doesn't move at all."

Defense Is Not Dumb

THE MACHIAVELLI PLAN

The question of whether or not the United States should finance political parties abroad through the CIA doesn't seem to be a problem to the administration. The only debate is about what parties should receive the money. Rumor has it that the CIA plans to give $6,000,000 to the Christian Democrats in Italy to make sure the Communists don't get elected. But there are some people in Washington who feel that now that the cat is out of the bag, the contribution could be counterproductive.

One of them is my friend Giulio Machiavelli, who knows the political situation in Italy as well as anybody.

"I think we should give money to a political party in Italy only if we're certain it will produce results."

"You mean to the Christian Democrats?" I said.

"No, I mean to the Italian Communist Party."

"Have you gone mad?" I said to Machiavelli. "Why would we give money to the Italian Communist Party?"

"It's very simple. If the CIA hands over the funds to the Italian Communist Party, everyone will say the Communists in Italy work for the CIA and the center parties will win the election."

"But that's Machiavellian," I told my friend. "The American people would never stand for it."

"Neither would the Italians," Machiavelli said. "Look,

right now every political party but the Communists are tainted in Italy because it is widely believed their politicians are on the CIA payroll. The only way we can reverse this is by putting the Communists on the payroll and cutting off everyone else."

"But you can't cut off non-Communist politicians from CIA funds," I protested. "The right, the center, and the non-Communist left depend on that money for their own personal expenses. They have villas to pay off, new cars to buy, Swiss bank accounts to keep up. You can't take money out of their pockets just to defeat the Communists."

"Ah, but that's just the point," Machiavelli said. "They won't be cut off. When the Soviets find out the CIA is supporting the Communist Party in Italy, the KGB will have no choice but to support the Christian Democrats. If we're to believe our government, the Soviets pour in a lot more money for an election in a foreign country than the Americans do, and therefore, the Christian Democrats will have more funds to salt away for themselves than when they were financed by the CIA."

"It's an interesting proposal," I said. "But what happens if the CIA financing is so successful the Communists win in Italy?"

"There is very little chance of that happening. In almost all cases whichever side the CIA supports in an election loses. But we must make sure that there is a great deal of publicity that the Communists in Italy are being financed by the Central Intelligence Agency."

"How would you publicize something like that?"

"We'd get Director George Bush to brief a congressional watchdog committee in secret session that the CIA was going to give six million dollars to the Italian Communist Party. He would make them all swear that they wouldn't reveal a word of it to anyone.

"Five minutes after the briefing was over every newspaper bureau in Washington would know about it. The day after the story was printed the White House would deny it. As soon as the denial came out, everyone in Italy would believe it was true."

"It's brilliant," I told Machiavelli. "But if the CIA starts supporting Communist parties in other countries, won't it hurt détente?"

"It might," he replied, "but what better way to show the Soviets that we mean business?"

MEDICAL ADVERTISING IS ALMOST HERE

The Federal Trade Commission (FTC) has attacked the American Medical Association (AMA) for illegal price fixing. It also says doctors keep patients from getting medical information by forbidding AMA members to advertise.

The big question raised by this attack is what kind of advertising the public will be exposed to if the FTC wins its case.

My friend Beezlebub, who owns an advertising agency, has already been working on some campaigns and hopes to garner a lot of accounts as soon as medical advertising becomes legal. He gave me a preview of what he had worked up.

First he showed me a large full-page ad for a newspaper with a black headline on the top: SPECIAL GEORGE WASHINGTON BIRTHDAY SALE ON ALL MAJOR OPERATIONS.

Madman Dr. Kelly announces the greatest surgery bargain in history. The first 100 people who show up at the Wesley Heights Clinic on George Washington's Birthday will be given a complete operation, including anesthesia and postoperative care, for $2.

Yes, for only $2 you could be lucky enough to have any organ in your body removed at once-in-a-lifetime prices.

Other Bicentennial bargains Madman Dr. Kelly is giving away include a brain operation for $14.95, a kidney transplant for $29.50, and a complete blood transfusion for $3.95.

If you can find a doctor in town who will charge less, Madman Dr. Kelly will give you FREE, yes, we said FREE, a plastic surgery nose job. Don't forget for one day only the greatest surgical sale in history at Madman Dr. Kelly's. No phone orders, please.

"How do you like it?" Beezlebub asked me.

"It's a heck of an ad," I admitted.

"Come on in the screening room. I want to show you some commercials my TV people worked out." Beezlebub pushed a button, and John Cameron Swayze came on the screen.

He was standing on the top of a cliff. "Ladies and gentlemen, I am standing on the highest cliff overlooking Acapulco. With me are two gentlemen, both of whom have had pacemakers implanted in their hearts. One was implanted by Dr. Wallace Welby. The other by a heart surgeon who charges three times what a Welby implant costs. We're going to do a little experiment now. Are you ready, gentlemen?"

The men nod.

John Cameron Swayze pushes both men off the cliff, and they plunge 300 feet to the rocks below.

The commercial picks up Swayze at the bottom, standing over their bodies. A doctor with a stethoscope is listening to their hearts.

"Well, Doctor?"

"This man's pacemaker is still working. This other man's heart has stopped." Swayze pulls off a bandage on the body of the man whose pacemaker is still working. The camera zooms in on a tattoo which reads "Welby, M.D."

Swayze looks out at the audience. "This proves you don't need an expensive doctor to insert a pacemaker. Dr. Welby is cheap in price, but not in work. Call this toll-free number today. Dr. Welby's pacemakers start at thirty-nine fifty, including installation and a three-month guarantee."

"I like it," I told Beezlebub.

"Here's one which I call the average-woman-type commercial." He pushed a button.

A man with a microphone is standing in a large doctor's office. In the background are three women on couches.

He goes over to the ladies. "Now, ladies, we're going to have some fun today. We're going to blindfold you and have you analyzed by three psychiatrists. After they're finished, I want you to tell me which one you liked the best."

A sign flashes on the screen which says, AFTER 50 MINUTES.

"All right, ladies, which doctor did you prefer?"

The first lady, after her blindfold is taken off, says, "I liked number two. He had a nice soft voice."

"Number two," the second lady says. "He seemed to understand my problem."

The third lady says, "I don't know who he is, but I'm switching to number two."

The announcer says, "And now, let's see who number two is. It's Dr. Adolph Fremluck, America's favorite psychiatrist. Yes, folks, everyone is switching to Dr. Fremluck, not only for the quality of his work but for his low fees. If you are depressed, paranoid, schizoid, or just plain neurotic, Dr. Fremluck has a cure for you. He's open every night until ten, and if you take advantage of his special January blues rates, he will give you absolutely free a set of Walt Disney coffee mugs with Mickey and Minnie, Donald Duck, and all the other characters that made your childhood so miserable. Don't delay. If you're sick in the head, Fremluck wants to hear from you today.

MARK I CAT FUTCH

The skipper of the submarine *Finback* was reprimanded last week for letting a topless go-go dancer named Cat Futch perform on the deck of his sub as it set sail from Port Canaveral for a three-month stint in the Atlantic.

Commander Connelly D. Stevenson defended his action on the grounds he was trying to help the morale of his men who had worked eighty-five hours a week to get their ship ready for the tour.

I have it on highest authority that after its hasty decision the Navy is reconsidering the whole incident and is now studying the possibility of assigning one go-go dancer to each submarine as part of a new weapons system.

A meeting was held in the Pentagon last week.

"Gentlemen, this morning we will discuss the possibility of installing a go-go dancer on each one of our killer submarines."

A chief petty officer brought out a series of charts.

The admiral giving the briefing took his pointer. "This is the Mark I Cat Futch model, which has just been tested at sea and given high marks by our research and development people."

"What exactly is its mission?" another admiral asked as he concentrated on the chart.

"The Mark I Cat Futch will be placed in one of the missile containers forward of the conning tower. When an enemy ship is spotted, the U.S. sub will immediately surface and the skipper will push this button here, which will raise the go-go dancer to the deck. When the Mark I Cat Futch is in position, the skipper will activate a rock and roll record and the go-go dancer will automatically start to gyrate."

"To what purpose?" an assistant secretary of the navy wanted to know.

The admiral flipped the chart and showed a close-up of Cat Futch. "The dance should mesmerize the crew of the enemy ship, and while they watch with mouths agape, the skipper will zero in with his torpedoes and let them fly. After the ship is sunk, the go-go dancer will be returned to her pad and lowered back into a defused position until the next general quarters."

"It's devilishly clever," a rear admiral said. "The Russians have nothing like it."

"I don't think the Chinese do either," someone else said.

The admiral flipped the chart. "The importance of the Mark I Cat Futch is that it can be used in peacetime as well as war. As you know, many foreign countries have been reluctant to let us sail into their ports. But just think of the reception a U.S. naval vessel would get if there were a topless go-go dancer twisting from port to starboard as we steamed in and out of a harbor?"

"What a great way to show the flag!" an admiral exclaimed.

"All right," the assistant secretary of the navy said. "It's a viable weapon, but what will it cost?"

"The Mark I Cat Futch can be leased for fifty dollars a day."

"That's not bad."

"And the only other cost will be five million to refit each submarine."

"A steal," a rear admiral said.

"Have we allowed for inflation?"

"Of course. And we've also budgeted for overruns."

"How do we justify the Cat Futch to Congress?" an admiral asked.

The briefing officer retorted, "We're going to say it's our only way of keeping abreast of the Soviet navy."

HUNTING FOR BUSINESS

There has been criticism in Washington lately over defense contractors entertaining Pentagon officials at hunting lodges and other places of ill repute. Former Secretary of Defense Schlesinger in referring to Northrop's entertainment policies said, "We have seen only the tip of the iceberg."

The latest word is that one aircraft firm even hired *girls* to accompany the guests on their trips into the woods.

I have a lobbyist friend from an aerospace company who thinks the hunting-lodge scandal is overkill.

Milbank told me, "All we were trying to do was give our senior fighting men some rest and recreation, and now they're trying to hang us for it."

"What you say is probably true," I told him, "but you'll have to admit it doesn't look good in the papers that your company was flying high-ranking officers off to shoot pheasant, duck, and what have you, while you were trying to sell them rockets and airplanes."

"Do you think a hunting weekend is going to influence a general into buying a certain kind of rocket or airplane? We never even talked about rockets or planes. We never talked about business at all."

"What did you talk about?"

"We talked about our wives and how much we all missed them."

"War is hell," I said. "But I read in the newspapers that you provided not only hunting facilities for Pentagon officials and key staff members of the Armed Services Committee, but also female companionship."

"Someone had to do the cooking and the cleaning," he said defensively.

"I'm not doubting your word, but there are some Americans who think you were up to no good."

"Give me their names," Milbank said, "and I'll see that they're fed into a Pentagon computer."

"That's not the point," I replied. "The only thing this country has always prided itself on is the absolute separation of the military from the industrial complexes. Even something as innocent as a hunting weekend with call girls is enough to put this independence into jeopardy."

Milbank said, "Look at it this way. The enlisted men have the USO. The junior officers have the officers' clubs. But where can a general go to have fun? Where can he relax and forget the burdens and cares of leadership? By maintaining hunting lodges, we were doing the same thing for generals that Bob Hope was doing for privates. We were building morale."

"Tell me the truth, Milbank. After one of those weekends, have you ever got an order from the Pentagon?"

"Never. Well, almost never. Once I was out shooting with an Air Force general and he got a rabbit with a shotgun I had loaned him. He said, 'This is a helluva gun,' and I said, 'If you think that's a gun, you ought to see one of our AK Four Fifty Red Line missiles.' He didn't believe me so I set one up and launched it. Sure enough, we wasted a rabbit thirty miles away. That impressed him so much he called me Monday and ordered four thousand of them. If my general hadn't gone hunting that weekend, this country would have been deprived of one of the finest weapons in its arsenal."

"I would like to have seen that scene on *The Guns of Autumn*," I said.

"Well, I guess with all the adverse publicity we're going to have to shut down the hunting lodge for a while," Milbank said.

"What will you do instead?"

"We bought a massage parlor near Alexandria. I'd like to see the Defense Department make something out of that!"

DEFENSE IS NOT DUMB

The news that the Defense Department was handing out contracts to private firms to train soldiers and airmen in the Middle East to defend their oilfields against us shook me up a little.

But Muldoon over at the Pentagon told me not to worry.

"Why shouldn't I worry?" I said. "One day Kissinger says if the Arabs strangle us, we might have to take the oilfields, and the next day you people are announcing that you're handing out contracts to teach the oil producers how to cope with a foreign attack."

"We're not stupid," Muldoon said. "Of course we're training Arabs to defend themselves. But that's part of our overall strategy. We're teaching them how to shoot high so if they ever have to fire at our boys, they'll miss us."

"No kidding," I said.

"Look, we had to make a decision about a year ago. Do we train the oil-producing nations in the arts of modern warfare or do we let somebody else do it? The consensus was that it was better for us to get the contracts than the French or the Soviets. But obviously there was a risk involved. So our people decided to hire instructors who didn't know what they were doing. For example, we found one Air Force ordnance man who always loaded missiles on our planes backward so they would fire in the wrong direction. He's been put in charge of instructing Arab ordnance men on how to arm their planes.

"By luck we found a former second lieutenant who was washed out of the Air Force navigation program four times. He is teaching Arab air force instructors how to fly in bad weather."

"Fantastic," I said.

"We found a destroyer captain who ran his ship aground three times. We gave him the choice of a court-martial or heading up all naval ship-handling training programs in the Middle East."

"He was a good choice," I agreed. "Aren't you instructing a lot of Arabs in antitank warfare?"

"Of course. But we have an ex-colonel in charge of the program who has never known how to set a fuse. When he was in the U.S. Army, his outfit blew up four hundred antitank guns before the shells left their barrels."

"Where do you find these people?" I asked.

"We have a computer that can produce a foul-up in a matter of seconds. If we want a radar man to train troops in the use of antiaircraft missiles, we just punch in and we get our man. We just gave out a contract to an ex-major who shot down fourteen of our own planes during maneuvers last year. Our leading electronics expert, an ex-general, blew the circuits on all our SAC communications systems for forty-eight hours. He is now installing similar systems all along the Persian Gulf."

"You people are really on the ball," I said with admiration.

Muldoon was very defensive. "Everyone criticizes us for these training programs, and they don't think we know what we're doing. But, dammit, we're not a bunch of fatheads. Do you believe we'd do anything that would endanger our own military forces?"

"I hope not," I said.

"Guess who is in charge of writing all the technical military manuals we send abroad?"

"Tell me."

"Clifford Irving."

A JOB FOR SUPERMAN

"Henry, Cambodia is falling, Vietnam is in shambles. This is a job for Superman. Go to a telephone booth, and put on your blue suit."

"I'm not going to do it, Nancy. I'm fed up with being Superman."

"How can you say that, Henry? The whole world is depending on you to save it."

"Nobody appreciates anything I do anymore. I'm going to stay home and play dominoes."

"You can't sulk, Henry. Have you ever seen Superman refuse to go on a mission?"

"That's easy for you to say. But Superman never had to deal with Senator Jackson or the Democrats on the Hill. He never had to explain détente or what it means to lose our credibility among our allies. I've had it, Nancy. I'm hanging up the suit."

"You can't do it, Henry. What would President Ford do without you? What would President Thieu do without you?"

"It's no good, Nancy. It was fun being Superman when I could fly over Hanoi and bomb the city and mine the harbors and make incursions into Cambodia. But what good is it to be Superman if I can't punish anyone for violating the Paris peace accords? Sure, I'll go in the phone booth and I'll put on the damn suit. What do I do then?"

"You'll think of something, Henry. You always do. Maybe you could deliver more tanks and guns and planes to South Vietnam so they could stop the onslaught of godless Communism."

"You need money for that—seven hundred million to be exact. Where am I going to get it? Congress won't give it to me, and we can't find any more accounting errors at the Pentagon. I'm sorry, Nancy, I'm sticking around the house for a while."

"It's not like you to be so down, Henry. The trouble is that you've been wearing street clothes, and no one has been taking you seriously. If you put on your Superman outfit and went up on the Hill, Congress would give you anything you wanted."

"You think so?"

"I'm sure of it, Henry. When you fly over the Capitol and land on the Senate Foreign Relations Committee's windowsill, they'll have no choice but to vote you all the military power you need to convince the North Vietnamese they made a big mistake when they underestimated the will of the American people's commitment to Indochina."

"All right, I'll give it a try. Where's the suit?"

"I just had it laundered and pressed."

(Ten minutes later)

"Nancy, I'm calling from the phone booth. The suit seems to have shrunk in the laundry. It doesn't fit anymore."

"That's because you've been putting on so much weight at those state dinners in the Middle East. Are you sure you can't get into it?"

"I ripped the seat trying to put it on. I'll look awfully funny going up to Congress with the back of it torn."

"Can you fly home? I'll sew it up."

"I'll try."

(Three minutes later)

"I'm not going, Nancy, no matter what you say."

"Why not, Henry?"

"Because as I was flying back to the house, everyone looked up and said, 'It's a bird! It's a plane!'—and then they laughed and said, 'No, it's Henry Kissinger with a big rip in the seat of his pants!' "

ROLL, JORDAN, ROLL

Washington went into a tailspin when King Hussein of Jordan refused to accept 532 Hawk surface-to-air missiles that the United States urged him to buy.

Hussein was angry because he said the United States had attached conditions to the sale. And Henry Kissinger was worried because Jordan could upset his Missiles for Peace game plan.

This is what was going on at the State Department during last week's crisis.

"Mr. Secretary, this cable just arrived from Jordan. Hussein is very upset because someone told him he could only use the Hawk missiles we're selling him for defensive purposes. He said he's never been so insulted in his life."

"Who told him he could only have them for defensive purposes?"

"I don't know, sir. Some damn fool who wasn't clued in on the big picture."

"Well, fire him. We can't have our State Department people telling foreign leaders when they can shoot our missiles in the air."

"Yes, sir."

"This is very serious. Do you realize if King Hussein refuses our missiles, then Israel could refuse them, and then Egypt could become suspicious and would not buy any, followed by Saudi Arabia, Yemen, and Abu Dhabi? My whole Middle East peace plan is based on everyone buying American missiles.

"Not to mention planes, tanks, and spare parts. If we allow Hussein to get away without buying the Hawk missiles, it will upset the military balance in the area. How can we justify selling Israel so many missiles if Hussein doesn't take any?

"You'd better get me King Hussein on the phone. . . . Your Highness, Henry here. . . . What do you mean he doesn't want to speak to me? . . . Tell him I'm sorry he feels insulted and that's what I'm calling about. . . . Thank you. . . . Ah, Your Highness, it's good to hear your voice. . . . Now please, Your Highness, there's been a misunderstanding. . . . That's right, I told you you could have the Hawk missiles with no strings attached. . . . There aren't any strings attached. . . . We have this stupid law passed by Congress that U.S. weapons can only be sold to countries who need them for defense. . . . You know how they are. They don't want someone to start a war for no reason at all. . . . Of course, I know you wouldn't start a war. . . . Sure, I trust you. . . . We trust everyone in that area. . . . Do you think we'd sell weapons to people we didn't trust? . . .

"Wait, wait. . . . Listen to me. All you have to do is promise us you won't use any of the Hawks offensively or transfer them to another country. . . . It's just a formality. Do you think we're going to come into your country and say, 'Hussein, what did you do with the missiles?'

"Your Highness, have I ever lied to you? Once you buy them, they're yours to do with as you like. You can shoot them all off on New Year's Eve for all we care. . . . I know the Russians have offered to sell you SAM missiles, but they're no match to the Hawk. Our Hawks will give you twice the bang for the buck. . . . It's in this month's *Consumer Reports*. . . .

"I'll tell you what. If you take the Hawks, we'll throw in three million dollars' worth of Red Eye shoulder-fired rockets and a brand-new ninety-million-dollar Vulcan antiaircraft gun system. . . . No, you don't have to accept any bribes from Lockheed or Northrop. . . . We'll make this one a straight sale. . . .

"I don't want to beg, Your Highness, but your accep-

tance of a multimillion-dollar arms deal from the United
States means a lot to me. . . . As a friend I'm asking
you, please take them. . . . You'll think it over? Thank
you, thank you from the bottom of my heart. . . . I
don't know how I can ever repay you. . . . Good-bye."

"Do you think he'll take them, sir?"

"He'd better—or we'll never have peace in our time."

NO DEFENSE FOR NEW YORK

"Mr. President, are you ready for this morning's briefing?"

"Yes, Henry, go ahead."

"Congress has just passed a bill making it possible for
us to give arms to Turkey."

"Good. How much do you think we should give them?"

"Maybe five hundred million dollars to start with. Those
bases mean a lot to us."

"It's a steal."

"We've just made a deal with Spain for air and naval
bases over the next five years."

"That's nice. What will it cost us?"

"I would say between six and seven hundred and fifty
million dollars over the next five years. They wanted two
billion dollars in military aid, but we put our foot down."

"I'm glad you did. We can't throw money around."

"We hope to get the two billion dollars for Israel and
the seven hundred fifty million dollars for Egypt before
the end of the congressional session."

"I should think so."

"We're getting a little resistance on the defense budget
from Congress. We asked for one hundred twenty billion
dollars, but the House only wants to give us one hundred
eleven billion dollars."

"Dammit, don't they realize such reductions are a sure
way to make us number two in a world where only
number one counts?"

"I warned them about that, sir, but you know how they are on the Hill. They never think about being number one."

"I'm going to have to go out to some more Republican fund-raising dinners and warn the American people that Congress is playing fast and loose with national security."

"I think you should, sir. The people want to see you, and they want to hear what you're up against."

"What else do you have to tell me?"

"The Treasury revised the U.S. deficit figures from sixty billion dollars to seventy billion dollars and possibly ninety billion dollars at the rate we're borrowing money."

"Well, it can't be helped. We need a strong economy, and we can't do it with a balanced budget."

"There's one more thing. Mayor Beame is in the outer office to see you about a loan for New York City."

"That's ridiculous! How does he expect the United States to loan him any money?"

"He's offering you U.S. air and naval bases. He claims his are better than the ones we have in Turkey and Spain. He says he'll give you the Brooklyn Naval Yard, La Guardia Field, and Staten Island on a long-term lease."

"That's outrageous! We're not going to finance Beame just because he has military bases we need."

"He also said he is willing to pull his troops back from the George Washington Bridge and out of the Lincoln Tunnel in exchange for two billion dollars in aid."

"Beame thinks he can get out of his fiscal problems by scaring us with war with New Jersey. But it isn't going to work. If he gets away with it, we'll be blackmailed by every mayor in America."

"Exactly my feelings, sir. We can't play sugar daddy for every bankrupt city in the country."

"Right, Henry, we've got to draw the line somewhere. Is that it?"

"South Korea wants seven hundred fifty billion dollars to beef up their defenses."

"Well, give it to them, for heaven's sakes. If we don't help our friends, who will?"

Let's Make a Treaty

FINGERING GUN CONTROL

The House Judiciary Committee in its infinite wisdom sent the latest handgun control bill back to a subcommittee for further "revision," thus probably killing it for another year. After a committee vote of 18 to 14 to send it to the floor, the National Rifle Association put on so much pressure that three congressmen reversed their previous positions, and that was the end of this year's hope for a safer and saner America.

When my friend Mindermann heard the news on the radio he called me. "You owe me five dollars. I told you Congress was too yellow to pass a gun control bill."

"That is not nice to say. The committee probably voted their consciences," I said.

"Yeah, right after they got the mailgrams from the NRA. Listen, you're living in a dream world if you think Congress is ever going to pass any kind of handgun control law."

"I can always hope," I said.

"The trouble with you bleeding hearts is that you're going about it the wrong way. You're trying to outlaw weapons that are as sacred to an American as underarm deodorants. You have to figure out some way of letting the people keep their guns, but at the same time do no harm to anyone."

"What do you suggest, wise guy?" I asked Minder-mann.

"Well, you're going to think I'm crazy, but I have an idea. You cut off everybody's trigger finger at birth."

"You are crazy."

"Hear me out. We can't do anything with the present generation, but we can save future generations from killing each other through accidents and anger and despair."

"But you can't cut off someone's trigger finger at birth," I protested.

"Why not? The Constitution gives everyone the right to bear arms, which is the main argument the NRA throws at us all the time. But there is nothing in the Constitution that says an American has to have ten fingers."

"But, Mindermann," I said, "it sounds so gory."

"It's a simple operation. Any doctor can perform it. The baby would never know it. When he got old enough, the parents could explain to him or her that since Congress would never pass a law prohibiting the manufacture and sale of guns, the only road open to them was to pass one forbidding any American to have a trigger finger."

"But the gun manufacturers and the NRA would be up in arms if you tried something like that."

"Why would they? We're not saying they can't sell guns or ammunition. They can do anything they damn please."

"But what good would a gun or ammunition be if no one has a finger to squeeze the trigger?"

Mindermann said, "Now you're getting the point. Listen, I've researched this thing. I took a poll of the House Judiciary Committee and the Senate, and not one of them had any strong feeling about fingers. There is no finger lobby to speak of. In fact, everyone I talked to said they couldn't see any reason for their constituents to object to having one finger removed, provided the government paid for it under Medicare."

"I'll have to admit it sounds simpler than trying to get a handgun control bill through Congress."

"It's the only answer to the problem," Mindermann said. "The slogan for the bill would be, 'If you can't take the trigger out of the gun, take the trigger finger out of the boy.'"

"I'll make a deal with you, Mindermann. I'll suggest it in my column, but you have to answer the mail."

"Deal. And don't forget to send the five dollars."

ARMED FORCES UNION 103

There is a lot of talk that American unions are seriously considering organizing members of the armed forces. Rumor has it that the unionization of military personnel will begin at the end of the year.

I can't see anything wrong with this, except that if the unions in the military get into job classifications it may be harder for our soldiers, sailors, and marines to fight another war.

Had our fighting boys been organized during World War II this is what might have happened.

The scene is aboard a battleship. It has been hit by the Japanese, and several sailors have been knocked out of action.

A chaplain realizes the seriousness of the situation and starts passing shells to the gunners as he sings "Praise the Lord and Pass the Ammunition."

The shop steward comes up to him. "I'm sorry, Padre, but you can't pass shells to the gunner. You're not a member of the Ammunition Carriers' Local Number 4."

"But," the chaplain says, "there aren't enough men to pass the ammunition so we'll all be free."

"That's the Navy's fault. They didn't hire enough carriers. By passing shells to the gunner, you are taking a job away from someone who needs it. The union rules specifically say that chaplains must pray, and that's it."

"All right, give me my Bible and I'll start to pray."

"I can't touch your Bible. Only members of the Boatswains' Union can move a Bible from one place to another."

"Oh, for God's sake. All right, I'll sing 'Praise the Lord and Pass the Ammunition.' "

"I'm sorry, Padre, if you're going to sing, you'll need at least ten musicians, and since this action is taking place at night, they will have to be paid overtime after midnight."

"We're at general quarters. Where am I going to get ten musicians?"

"You can use a phonograph, but you'll have to pay for a standby orchestra."

"It doesn't seem to make any difference," the chaplain says, "we're sinking. I'm putting on my life jacket."

"You can't put on your life jacket, Padre. Members of the Deckhand Dressers' Guild are the only ones who can put on your life jacket for you."

"When the ship sinks, is it all right to swim?"

"Yes, but if you get into a lifeboat, you can't row. That job classification has been given to the Pastry Chefs' Local 135."

The soldiers may also find themselves in trouble. Corporal Barney McNeil is manning a machine gun at Bastogne. As each wave of Germans attack, McNeil fires away, dropping them in their tracks. Sergeant Roy Bender, shop steward for the Machine Gun and Mortar Firers' Union, crawls over to him.

"What do you think you're doing, Barney?"

"I'm killing Germans," Barney says, letting another blast go.

"You're killing too many Germans!" Bender shouts at

him. "Slow up, or the other guys will think you're an eager beaver. Our contract says we're not supposed to kill more than ten Germans a day. I can see a hundred bodies over there."

"But, dammit, we have to win the war," Barney protests.

"Listen, you dope, if you kill one hundred Germans in an hour, the Army will expect us all to kill one hundred Germans in the same time. Relax, go have a cigarette or get into a crap game somewhere. In an hour we'll go into overtime, and then you can kill some more Germans if you want to."

"Bull ----, I'm going to win me a Congressional Medal of Honor," Barney says.

"You try it, and I'll bring you up on charges with the union board. They can fine you three months' pay for winning a medal and making the rest of us look bad."

"Here they come again!" Barney says, raking the horizon with bullets.

Sergeant Bender is hit in the shoulder by a German fragment. "I'm hit, Barney! Stop the bleeding."

"I'm sorry, Sarge. If I touched you, the Corpsmen's Union would never forgive me."

WHAT HAPPENED TO REFORM?

When the new Congress was elected in 1974, there was a great deal of publicity about the Young Turks that were going to bring about reform in the legislative branch of government. A few people may have wondered what reforms they produced and what happened to these tough young men and women who were going to go up against the system.

One, whom I'll call Efrem Haldibird, told me.

"It wasn't as easy to fight the system as I thought it would be."

"What happened?"

"Well, what we didn't know was Congressman Wayne Hays of Ohio was in charge of the House Administration Committee."

"What has that got to do with reform?"

"Everything. If you go up against the system, you don't get a parking space on the Hill. How can anyone serve the people if he can't park at the Capitol? You may think election reform is very important to this country, but it certainly doesn't have priority over parking."

"So the reason the Young Turks haven't made any inroads in Congress is that if they tried to do anything, they would lose their parking privileges."

"It wasn't just parking privileges. Some of us could have lived with that. But Hays is also in charge of office expenses. If we went up against him, we might have found ourselves without pencils. How can you write new reforms if you don't have any pencils?"

"Typewriters?" I suggested.

"Hays is in charge of typewriters, too. If he gets mad at you, you could wind up with a really lousy typewriter. It's one thing to want to change things in the House, but how can you do it if you don't have the tools to work with?"

"Hays has you in a box."

"He can put you in one if he wants to. He's in charge of allocating office space. If you're not willing to play the game, you can wind up talking to your constituents in the men's room."

"That's tough when the League of Women Voters comes to town," I said. "But what are you going to do this election after you promised the people in your district that if you were elected, you would bring about much-needed reforms in Washington?"

"I'm going to talk about furniture. What I didn't know when I ran in 1974 is that if you don't become a team player, the old-timers can really screw you up on getting decent furniture for your office. I know one member of the freshman caucus who stuck to his guns on an issue Wayne Hays was against, and his swivel chair collapsed on him right in the middle of an important committee hearing. He got the message pretty fast."

"Are you trying to tell me that the reason the freshman caucus hasn't been heard from the past year is that they're afraid Wayne Hays will see they get faulty furniture?"

"Of course not. It's really the stationery problem. You see, he's in charge of how much stationery we get. If he cut down our stationery allotment, all of us would be in serious trouble. We can sit on rotten chairs with the stuffing coming out of them, but you take away our stationery and we're in serious trouble."

"I can appreciate that."

"He also has to authorize our travel vouchers. No one in this country is going to mess around with someone who authorizes his travel vouchers. That's suicide."

"Well, I'm glad you explained it to me. I thought you had just lost interest in trying to reform the system."

"That's ridiculous. We're as determined as ever to make this body more responsible to the people's needs. But we can't do it unless we have an adequate supply of paper clips."

THE SECRET FACTORY

Probably the biggest business in Washington is the manufacturing of secrets. In the past twenty years the demand for secrets has increased tenfold, and because the government cannot keep up with it, all federal agencies are now subcontracting their orders for secrets to private industry.

I visited one of these secret manufacturing factories the other day. It is called Hush Hush Limited and is located in a suburb outside Washington, D.C.

Arnold Zankel, one of the founders of the company, was my escort.

"We're going twenty-four hours a day," he said proudly. "Everyone in the government is desperate for secrets, and they all need them immediately."

"I thought the CIA hearings and the disclosures about the FBI and the Watergate scandal would have hurt your business."

"*Au contraire,*" said Zankel. "As soon as a secret is revealed to the public, the agency involved orders a new one to replace it. The demand for full disclosure of what the government is up to has made every government department search for more sophisticated secrets that can't be discovered."

Zankel took me into a large room which was completely automated. There were machines typing up documents and other machines stamping them "Confidential."

"This is our bread and butter business," he explained. "We supply eighty percent of all the confidential papers used by the federal government."

"How do they order them?"

"By the ton. We might get a call from HEW or HUD and they'll say we need three tons of confidential papers for the week."

"Don't they specify what kind they want?"

"No, confidential papers do not have a high rating in the government, but it does make the department look good to have them in their files. So nobody really cares what's on them. We just program our electric typewriters to type up anything that looks official, then we stamp them 'Confidential,' bale them in hundred-pound packages, send them over by truck, and throw them on the steps of the agency every morning."

We came to some swinging doors. "This is something that might interest you," Zankel said. The large, airy room had three long tables at which were seated men and women in white smocks. They were working on binding volumes of mimeographed papers.

"What are they doing?"

"They're binding secrets to be subpoenaed. These are secrets that can be given to congressional committees."

I looked perplexed.

Zankel explained, "Congress is demanding more and more secrets from the executive branch of the government. So we are manufacturing secrets especially tailored to satisfy congressional subpoenas. For example, these chips have been ordered by the Federal Reserve Board and have to do with the private affairs of banks. When Congress demands to see the secret papers in the Fed's files, the Federal Reserve Bank will send these over. Obviously, they're so complicated that no one can understand them. But since they have a lot of bulk to them, the committees are usually satisfied. The people over there are working on energy secrets, and down there they are dealing with agricultural exports. Our job is to see that no one can make head or tail out of them."

Before we went into the next room, Zankel made me put on rubber boots. We entered a hall with three inches of water on the floor.

"This is probably our most difficult work. We have to make secrets here that can be leaked."

"You have government orders for secrets that leak?" I asked in surprise.

"It's one of our biggest items. High government officials are constantly leaking secrets to the press and pretending surprise that the secret got out. We've developed a container which can hold a secret in a solid state until the word goes out it should be leaked. Then, by just twisting this tab, the secret becomes soluble and leaks all over town."

"Fantastic," I said.

"It's our biggest item. Between Henry Kissinger, Pat

Moynihan, and the congressional committee investigating the CIA, we can't keep them in stock."

LET'S MAKE A TREATY

The United States recently signed a new military treaty with Spain. In exchange we will, of course, supply the Spanish with armaments so we can keep our bases there.

It seems that we can't make a deal with any country without giving them arms in exchange for friendship. There is a suspicion that the State Department has been influenced by all the TV game shows and it seems to me that since the American people pay for most of the military aid, we should at least be permitted to watch the United States hand out the stuff on television in a game show format.

This is just a suggestion. Every week the State Department would produce a TV program called *Let's Make a Treaty*.

The secretary of state would be the master of ceremonies, and the audience would be made up of ambassadors from all the countries of the "free world."

He would call out a number, and the ambassador from that nation would jump up on the stage.

Henry would say, "Where are you from, sir?"

"Zambia," the ambassador would reply excitedly. (Applause).

"All right. I'm going to ask you a question. If you can answer it correctly, I will give you a hundred million dollars. Are you ready?"

The ambassador, jumping up and down, says, "Yes, yes."

"The question is: 'Who is the President of the United States?' "

The ambassador hesitates. "Jerry Ford?"

"That is correct!" Henry shouts, and he counts out

$100,000.000. The ambassador hugs and kisses the secretary of state as the audience goes wild.

"Now don't go away," says the secretary. "You can keep the one hundred million or give it back to me in exchange for what is behind one of the three curtains over there. Joan Braden, will you tell us some of the prizes that are behind the curtains?"

"Sir, we have the new version of the Hawk missile, a 1976 Super Sherman tank, a year's supply of cruise missiles, a complete nuclear energy plant which will be installed absolutely free, and a squadron of F-15 fighter planes."

"All right, Mr. Ambassador," the secretary says, "do you want to keep the one hundred million, or do you want to go for the prizes behind the curtains?"

The ambassador, clutching the money, looks out at the audience. "Keep the money," some ambassadors scream. Others yell, "Go for the curtain."

The ambassador says to the secretary, "Can I consult with my government?"

"I'm sorry, we don't have time. What's it going to be?"

The ambassador hands back the $100,000,000. "I'll go for what's behind the curtain."

The audience applauds loudly.

"All right," the secretary says. "He's going for what's behind the curtain. We have curtain number one, curtain number two, and curtain number three. Which one will you choose?"

The ambassador hesitates as the audience shouts out, "TWO!" "ONE!" "THREE!"

Finally, he says, "Curtain number three."

The curtain opens, and there is a pile of rotten wheat. The audience groans.

"Well, Mr. Ambassador, it looks like you made a mistake. But since you've been such a good sport, we've got a consolation prize for you. Joan, what's the consolation prize?"

Ms. Braden pushes away the pile of rotten wheat, and behind it is a brand-new nuclear submarine.

The secretary of state, grinning, says, "You gave up one hundred million in cash, but you have won a new nuclear submarine which is worth four hundred and fifty million! Here are the keys to it."

The audience goes crazy as the ambassador jumps up and down and rushes over to the nuclear submarine and climbs up on the conning tower.

The secretary, beaming, says to the audience, "Well, that's it for tonight, folks. If you are an accredited member of any freedom-loving country in the world and you would like to be on *Let's Make a Treaty,* write to me at the State Department for tickets. All the prizes given away on this program were donated through the courtesy of the American taxpayer in the interests of world peace. Thank you, God bless you, and we'll see you all next week."